The Librarian's Genealogy Notebook

A Guide to Resources

DAHRL ELIZABETH MOORE

AMERICAN LIBRARY ASSOCIATION
Chicago and London
1998

Dahrl Elizabeth Moore is university librarian at Florida Atlantic University, Boca Raton. She was awarded the Master in Library Science degree in 1980 from the University of South Florida. In 1986, she received the Master of Arts in History degree from Florida Atlantic University. As president of the Palm Beach County Genealogical Society (1993 to 1995; 1997 to 1999), she lectures in various genealogical subjects for the society's workshops and seminars. In 1997, she taught as adjunct faculty "Library Resources for Genealogical Research" for the University of South Florida Library and Information Science Program. Since 1974, Moore has done extensive genealogical research in the United States, England, and Scotland. In addition, during her tenure as chair of the Genealogical and Local History Caucus for the Florida Library Association in 1992, she compiled and published *Historical and Genealogical Holdings in the State of Florida.*

While extensive effort has gone into ensuring the reliability of information appearing in this book, the publisher makes no warranty, express or implied, on the accuracy or reliability of the information, and does not assume and hereby disclaims any liability to any person for any loss or damage caused by errors or omissions in this publication.

Project editor: Eloise L. Kinney

Cover and text design: Lucy Lesiak Design

Cover genealogy art courtesy of Rebecca Strehlow

Printed on 50-pound Glatfelter, a pH-neutral stock, and bound in 10-point coated cover stock by Edwards Brothers

The paper used in this publication meets the minimum requirements of American National Standard for Information Sciences—Permanence of Paper for Printed Library Materials, ANSI Z39.48-1992. ⊗

Library of Congress Cataloging-in-Publication Data
Moore, Dahrl Elizabeth.
    The librarian's genealogy notebook : a guide to resources / Dahrl Elizabeth Moore.
      p.   cm.
    Includes bibliographical references (p.   ) and index.
    ISBN 0-8389-0744-X (acid-free paper)
    1. Genealogy.   2. United States—Genealogy—Handbooks, manuals, etc. I. Title
CS9.M66 1998
929'.1—dc21   98-19110

Printed in the United States of America.

02 01 00 99 98   5 4 3 2 1

Contents

Acknowledgments

I would like to thank all my students in the genealogy course for their positive feedback on the idea of this notebook. I would like to thank Malka Schyndel for her guidance and encouragement in seeing this project through to its finish and for giving me the confidence to know I could do such an undertaking. A big *thank you* is also due my three children—Frank, for helping with the computer programs and putting up with all my foolish questions; and John and Jeanne for being so supportive.

Introduction

The idea for this work came as a result of teaching a course on "Library Resources for Genealogical Research" to library students from the University of South Florida Library and Information Science East Coast Program. Many library school graduates will be working in a public or an academic library with little or no background in helping patrons requesting information on genealogy. This publication is designed to locate the many resources in any library, public or academic, that can help provide service to these patrons. As more and more people search for their family roots, they find libraries the place to start their search for their ancestors. The better equipped a librarian is to serve them, the better the relationship will be for both sides.

Genealogists are known to be very vocal in their desires for library service. The Genealogy Committee of the History Section of the Reference and Adult Services Division of the American Library Association (ALA) has issued *Guidelines for Developing Beginning Genealogical Collections and Services* (reprinted in *RQ*, v. 32, fall 1992, pp. 31–32).

A genealogy researcher's positive relationship with the library staff can be profitable on all sides. It could encourage the genealogy patrons to become part of the Friends of the Library and boost financial support for library programs. With shrinking budgets in many library systems, this is one very successful way to add additional items to the library collection. Another trend in some libraries is to house the genealogical collection of a local society that would have no other home. This section is usually serviced by volunteers from the society on a part-time basis, thus freeing regular staff for other duties during these hours.

As libraries differ in all parts of the country, this publication is designed to allow customization by each library. This will enable a library to make the most of state and local resources as well as provide coverage of national resources.

The book consists of materials that can be found in most libraries and how they can be used to answer many of the genealogical patrons' questions. Call numbers and locations in each library can be added after the titles. Samples of various forms, such as a five-generation chart and a family group sheet, are included in appendixes so the librarian has an idea of what they are. There is a brief classification scheme for Library of Congress (LC) and Dewey Decimal systems. The book also includes some information for customization by each library, additional national resources, and Internet web sites.

Academic libraries are beginning to find that more and more genealogy patrons are starting to make use of their holdings. These libraries are more likely to have the historical background material necessary to place an ancestor in time and place and make family history come alive. They will also usually have the more expensive reference tools needed to complete family research. Many archives and special collections in these academic institutions are proving to be gold mines for the family historian. Archives house personal papers, business historical papers, diaries, letters, pictures, and many other types of material. It is well worth knowing how to access this material.

Genealogy is now regarded as the third-largest hobby in the United States. This increased interest can be taxing on the staff and resources of libraries. Some of the drives for this interest are retirees with some time on their hands and broken families looking for family roots. Also, the opening of adoption records is encouraging adoptees to try to locate their birth families. Of course, the Internet is proving to be a boon for genealogy, with more information coming full-text online as well as having online journals for help tips, chat rooms for instant repartee, and thousands of links to genealogy resources. Librarians must know how to access these sources to provide the best possible service to these patrons. But they must also realize everything found on the Internet must be verified from other, more reliable sources. This cannot be stressed enough.

Obviously, this work will not address all the questions a genealogy patron could ask. It will provide some help and guidelines for the librarian to feel more at ease providing service to patrons and helping them start their own research. Localizing the pertinent information to each library location could aid in a better understanding of all resources in and around each library.

Brief Introduction to Genealogy and Family History

Genealogy and *family history.* What do we mean by these terms and how do they differ? Genealogy is the study of the descent from one ancestor in a direct line to another by verifying birth, marriage, and death dates. This would make a great fifteen-generation chart if it were all filled in, but it would still be pretty dull reading.

Family history, however, broadens our understanding of who our ancestors were; how and where they lived, worked, and traveled; and how you can relate to them with a little better understanding of who you are. In other words, family history puts flesh on the skeleton of dates that genealogy uncovers. This would be rewarding not only for the individual researcher, but for all the family and would leave a legacy for future generations.

The latest surge of interest in genealogy began with the U.S. bicentennial in 1976, and this was followed by Alex Haley's book, *Roots.* The television series based on *Roots* had some of the highest ratings of any program in the history of television. We are still seeing the continued interest in genealogy, and with computer programs, the World Wide Web (WWW), e-mail access, and the Internet helping to aid in research, there does not seem to be a letup in sight.

HOW TO BEGIN: A GUIDE FOR LIBRARIANS AND RESEARCHERS

Genealogy research should always begin with yourself and work backward to your parents, grandparents, and so forth. Collect the items in your own life that have meaning to you. Start with your birth certificate, pictures of yourself as you grew, diplomas, and yearbooks. Write down your memories of travels, visits to grandparents, and where you lived, with memories—fond or otherwise—of the houses you lived in, your favorite places in the town where you grew up, and so on.

Once you do this, it will give you a perspective on the type of information you need to collect for your parents, grandparents, great-grandparents, and so forth. Doing this also gives more meaning to who you are and where you came from and maybe some understanding of how you developed.

Work with one generation at a time, and prove each step along the way. Check with all your living relatives and record their memories. This can be accomplished with the aid of a tape recorder or video camera, being sure to note time, place, and person being interviewed and the interviewer. Your relatives' memories may be able to give you a start as relatives often know facts, locations, and relationships, even though some of this may be a bit vague. They also might have family records, photographs, and Bibles that they will be willing to share to help you get started. The photographs should be identified if at all possible. Do *not* write on the photograph itself. If possible, put it in an acid-free sheet protector and label that. Be sure to record their family stories and remembrances as there just might be enough facts for you to work on to go further in your research.

An example: I have a story written by my husband's father about the stories he remembered his father and grandfather told him when he was a child. His grandfather was a sea captain, and at this time they were living in Nebraska, a long way from the sea. You can imagine how fascinating these stories must have been to a small child who probably never saw more than a stream or river. I have been documenting this story and found that a year or two in the chronology might be off, but basically the story has proved to be a bonus in ferreting out the genealogy of this Moore family. Such remembrances could take you back two and three generations with little time and effort, as this story did for me.

As you go back, you will come to a time when there was no television, radio, indoor plumbing, automobiles, or electric lights, among other things. What did your ancestors do for play? How did they travel? What was school like? How did they dress? Did they shop using a Sears catalog? If libraries have copies of old Sears catalogs, you can find pictures of clothing, household wares, and other items from specific time periods. Check old newspapers for ads, which will also give you pictures of this same type of thing. What were their occupations? (I was fortunate that I had an aunt who wrote a brief story of her early life and what emotions she felt with the advent of indoor plumbing, electric lights, radio, and television. Her first memory of indoor plumbing was scary. The bathroom was located in the basement, between the furnace and the coal bin, and she was reluctant to go down the stairs when the furnace was roaring. These were momentous events in her life as she grew to old age and ones she never forgot.)

You need to know full names, dates, and places of birth, marriage, death, and burial and other significant background that helps round out the family tree. Remember that each generation will *double* the number of relatives you have (i.e., two parents, four grandparents, eight great-grandparents, sixteen great-grandparents, and so on).

Each entry on your family group record will need documentation as to where you received your information. You can not rely on a previously printed genealogy as gospel truth. Many of the earlier works were not documented, and people continued to print erroneous information time after time, accepting whatever information was uncovered with no thought to verify any of it. (The Daughters of the American Revolution (DAR) are now finding several of their members were accepted under false papers and are now requiring more stringent proof of a lineage before accepting any new member.) The Board of Certification of Genealogists requires rigid guidelines in research methodology before accepting new members. The bad reputation genealogy had among historians and social scientists through the years is now disappearing to a great extent because of these more stringent guidelines. Moreover, these same people are recognizing the very important work the genealogical field has done in preserving and publishing many of the records they also need in their research.

Types of Sources

There are two types of information—primary and secondary. *Primary sources* are those that involve someone directly involved with the event and are reported at the time of the event. Almost everything else is a *secondary source*. Birth and marriage records are considered primary sources if they were recorded at the time of the event and secondary sources depending on who recorded the event and when. A death record is usually a secondary source because someone else gives the basic information about the death. This information is usually given under adverse conditions of grief or lack of knowledge by the person giving the information. It may be from a spouse too grief stricken to remember clearly; from the children, who might or might not know exact dates and places; or from a family friend who knows even less. The cause of death is considered primary source information if the doctor is the one giving the information.

Other considerations in evaluating primary and secondary sources are the reliability of the person giving the information, the handwriting involved and how it is clarified, and how long after the event the information was recorded. It is up to you to evaluate the records as best you can, but record them nonetheless.

Organizing It All

In a short time you will have accumulated quite a bit of recorded information. To keep this information together, I would suggest three-ring binders with dividers for each head of the family, keeping each family together. Several publications explain how to number your ancestry. See Joan F. Curran, *Numbering Your Genealogy: Sound and Simple Systems*, National Genealogical Society Special Publications, no. 59 (Arlington, Va.: National Genealogical Society, 1992); or William Dollarhide, *Managing a Genealogical Project*, rev. and updated (Baltimore, Md.: Genealogical Publishing Co., 1991).

A computer program will help organize this information more efficiently. For a selection of computer-assisted materials, see section 16, on computer databases. Keep copies of all interviews you have with relatives, parents, and others by recording date, place, and person interviewed. A Research Calendar will keep you abreast of who you interviewed, sources used, and what information you collected (see appendix 1). Note all correspondence by using a Correspondence Calendar—you can make one yourself or buy one already printed. I made the one in appendix 2 and have used it a long time. This calendar should include date, where sent, type of information requested, any money sent, and when and what reply was received. This will keep you from duplicating your efforts and enable you to note at a glance where you are heading in your quest for information. Three main types of charts are available to help you organize your information: the ancestor chart, the family group record, and census extraction forms.

Ancestor Chart

These are also known as generation, or pedigree, charts and can record four, five, and up to fifteen generations, depending on the chart you purchase. This type of chart is like a road map through time and generations of lineal ancestors and can show at a glance where more research is needed (an example of a five-generation chart is found in appendix 3). Note on these charts that males are always even numbers and females are odd numbers. Dates should always be written in a standard format: 03 Jan 1998. Try to remember the "2, 3, 4" principle—2 for the day, 3 for the three-letter abbreviation for the month, and 4 for the full year—when recording dates, and soon it will become a habit. The full year is absolutely necessary. If "97" is used for year, it is very unclear whether it means for 1697, 1797, 1897, or 1997. By keeping to this format, there is no confusion about what year, day, or month is meant, as when using 1/3/98, as is done in the United States. The British and other Europeans would write this as 3.1.98, which could cause endless confusion in recording dates from their records.

Family Group Record

One such form should be filled out for each head of household and for each marriage, especially if there are children with each marriage (see appendix 4). Included are the father and mother, with her maiden name, and all the children. It is a good idea to get into the habit of writing the surname in capital letters (e.g., John DOE). If the maiden name of the wife is the same as that of the husband, always underline her surname to denote that fact. There is a space for the parents of each husband and wife. Children should be entered in order of birth, with all the pertinent information noted. Be *sure* to include the sex of each child. As you go back in time, it is sometimes very difficult to determine the sex by name alone. Be sure to include the source of information for each fact entered. I also use the back of the sheet to record this information.

Census Extraction Forms

These forms enable one to extract the information for the various census years accurately. (More on the census in section 4.) Forms for all census years from 1800 to 1920 are included in appendixes 5 through 14 for comparing information gathered.

Another aspect of genealogy that is very important is the ethnic background of the people involved. The *Random House Dictionary of the English Language* (New York: Random House, 1967), p. 489, gives these meanings for the word *ethnic*:

> 1. pertaining to or characteristic of a people, esp. to a speech or culture group. 2. referring to the origin, classification, characteristics, etc., of such groups. 3. pertaining to non-Christians. 4. belonging to or deriving from the cultural, racial, religious, or linguistic traditions of a people or country, esp. a primitive one.

The United States in the past has been called "a melting pot," implying that distinctions among people of different ethnic backgrounds were unimportant. Today, however, interests are more in preserving ethnic identities rather than blending into a homogenous whole. The eighteenth and nineteenth centuries brought millions of immigrants to U.S. shores, strongly represented in the urban and suburban areas, where ethnic flavor is more diverse than it is in rural areas, where populations remained relatively stable.

Depending on your area, you might want to investigate the ethnic groups that use your library or have a genealogical or historical society in your area. Certain areas of the country have a heavy population of Hispanics, Afro-Americans, Lithuanians, Poles, and so on. It would be a good idea to investigate sources for the different groups, as each group has special research methods. Here you will have to have good maps to locate each ancestor's birthplace. A world gazetteer will help locate the towns, villages, and borders when there is a question of location. Ports of departure are often difficult to ascertain and require extensive work with passenger lists. There are several books on the market that can help here, such as Ira A. Glazier and P. William Filby, eds., *Germans to America: Lists of Passengers Arriving at U.S. Ports, 1850–1893* (Wilmington, Del.: Scholarly Resources, 1988–). There is also an ongoing publication with multiple volumes: Ira Glazier and Michael H. Tepper, eds., *The Famine Immigrants: Lists of Irish Immigrants Arriving at the Port of New York, 1846–1851* (Baltimore, Md.: Genealogical Publishing Co., 1983–86). There are seven volumes to this set and an excellent index, with lists for Czech, Polish, English, Scottish, French, and many other immigrants. Check Marian Hoffman, ed., *Genealogical and Local History Books in Print*, 5th ed., 5 vols. (Baltimore, Md.: Genealogical Publishing Co., 1997), for other publications that would be pertinent to your library. *Illinois Libraries* devoted an entire issue to ethnic genealogical resources mainly in the Illinois area (vol. 74, no. 5, November 1992). Illinois libraries should keep a copy handy for referral.

Oryx Press has a series, *A Student's Guide to . . . Genealogy*, with twelve volumes that give lots of how-to help in dealing with the following ethnic groups: African American, British American, Chinese American, German American, Irish American, Italian American, Japanese American, Jewish American, Mexican American, Native American, Polish American, and Scandinavian American. These books can be purchased by the volume or the set. See section 12 for the address of Oryx Press.

There are many ethnic societies around the United States these days, and you might want to contact those in your area to find out their activities. Searching for the ethnic identity of an immigrant ancestor leads to emigration from one country and immigration into another. This encompasses passenger lists at both ends of travel. An ethnic genealogy society is more apt to have the specialized records or to know their locations. They also might be more familiar with the language, the names, and handwriting. In many countries certain names have a strong locality derivation and that can be of great help in discovering ancestral roots. Passenger records are discussed in section 5.

As you can see, genealogy encompasses becoming a detective, historian, confirmed snoop, ingrained diplomat, keen observer, hardened skeptic, apt biographer, linguist, part-time lawyer, accurate reporter, and dabbler in genetics. The study of genealogy and family history covers almost every field of knowledge, touches on all manner of records, encourages travel, develops patience, and produces a wealth of paperwork.

WARNING—GENEALOGY POX
Very Contagious to Adults

SYMPTOMS: Continual complaint as to need for names, dates, and places. Patient has blank expression, sometimes deaf to spouse and children. Has no taste for work of any kind, except feverishly looking through records at libraries and courthouses. Has compulsion to write letters. Swears at mail carrier when he or she doesn't leave mail. Frequents strange places such as cemeteries, ruins, and remote, desolate country areas. Makes secret night calls. Hides phone bills from spouse. Mumbles to self. Has strange, faraway look in eyes.

THERE IS NO KNOWN CURE!

TREATMENT: Medication is useless. Disease is not fatal but gets progressively worse. Patient should attend genealogy workshops, subscribe to genealogical magazines, and be given a quiet corner in the house where he or she can be alone.

REMARKS: The unusual nature of this disease is that the sicker the patient gets, the more he or she enjoys it.

ANONYMOUS

Library Reference Service

A word of caution: Helping a genealogy patron is really no different than helping any other patron searching for information. Genealogy is a legitimate subject of inquiry, and librarians, especially in public libraries, have no right to make value judgements on inquiries in their libraries or to refuse or show reluctance to assist any patron. Your positive attitude toward patrons can help establish their feeling at ease in the entire library experience and can have very positive results for both you and your patrons. Enough said.

KNOW YOUR OWN LIBRARY

First and foremost, know your own library. As you go around your stacks, make note of holdings that can be used for genealogy. Take down the title, call number, and location, whether in reference, government documents, children's collection, and so forth. Keep the list handy at the reference desk, or annotate the two reference bibliographies in sections 6 and 7.

There are a few other things a librarian can do to make a genealogist feel welcome and to ease concerns among the staff about dealing with these patrons. Find a member of your staff who will be willing to learn more about the genealogical process (if one is not doing genealogy already). Have this person give talks on your library and its holdings of genealogical material to local genealogical and historical societies. Arrange tours and exhibits of relevant materials for other librarians in your library. Be aware that other members of the staff might not have any interest or training in genealogical research. Encourage them by offering a minitraining session within the library. Compile and publish a guide to such material, as well as a layout of the library, locating copy machines and their charges, the reference section, the card catalog, restrooms, water fountains, and so forth.

Work with archivists and special collection librarians in university libraries in your area to know the types of material they collect, availability of use, and how it can be incorporated into your guides. If your library collects local history, find out about the holdings, give talks on the types of material collected and how they can be used, and set up displays to call attention to this material. If there is a local genealogy society in your area, request a talk on genealogy in your library for all the staff by one of the genealogists of the society. If there is a genealogy library in the area, request a tour of the facility to better understand the types of materials that are available. You will be surprised at the variety of material available and understand a bit better just what genealogists face when searching for that elusive ancestor, date, or place. Unless working on your own genealogy, this type of material will probably be new to you, and the better you become acquainted with it, the better you can help your patron.

REFERRAL

Unless your library has a large genealogical collection, for many librarians the assistance to genealogical inquiries will consist largely if not wholly in referral work, directing inquiries to other places where the information sought is or is likely to be found. Have such sources at the reference desk for quick reference. Do not refer patrons to a source unless you have the necessary backup information at hand (i.e., address, contact person's name, phone number, hours of operation, etc.) or know where to get it quickly.

REFERENCE INTERVIEW

I can not stress enough the importance of the reference interview. There are very necessary questions that one should keep in mind when trying to help genealogists. You have to ask questions as you would in any reference interview and try to draw out exactly what the patron wants to know. The patron might not be able to explain exactly what is wanted. When helping patrons, have them show you the chart they are working on to give you a better perspective of what type of information they are seeking. Have the patrons show you any other forms they are using and how these forms are filled out. Check to see what information is recorded, and the answers to the following questions will have more meaning.

Who
Who is the person they are searching? You must have a name, a full name if possible. It also helps if names of parents and siblings are known. Someone named John Smith would be rather hard to pin down in any time frame without knowing a bit more of the family and their location.

What
What do they hope to find? Are they searching for pension records, vital records, census records, passenger arrival records, military service records, naturalization records, or other records? The type of information wanted will determine the type of record searched.

Where
Where is the location of this person? In the United States, you need to know the state, county, city or town, and the time frame. As the United States grew, so did the states and counties, changing boundaries along the way.

In such countries as England, Germany, Ireland, and Canada, the same detail of information is a must. In foreign countries wars often changed national boundaries, depending on who won the conflict. The United Kingdom reorganized its counties in 1974, with many changing names and others merging into others. It is possible, then, to have to know of two sources and locations before doing any research there. Know where the maps and gazetteers are located for handy reference. The gazetteers will help you determine exact locations of towns and cities. Be sure to have older atlases available as well as up-to-date ones to show the boundaries of countries and how they have changed as well as the names of the countries themselves.

When

What time period is being considered? It is important to know what type of records to consult. Time periods in the United States include colonial, the Revolution, Civil War, and westward expansion, among others. These all have their own special resources. Colonial records are most often kept either in the towns themselves or in the state archives. After 1779, with the formation of the United States, such records are more often kept in the National Archives and Records Administration (NARA) and its branches. The National Archives is the national repository for all federal records. The archives do not have state or county records unless there is a direct relationship to the federal government. Some records were a carryover from the colonial period and can be found in the National Archives, but they are few in number in comparison to the rest of the records. For more information, see Howard H. Wehmann, comp., *A Guide to Pre-Federal Records in the National Archives,* revised by Benjamin L. DeWhitt (Washington, D.C.: National Archives and Records Administration, 1989).

Why

What is the objective this patron seeks? Patrons may seek to gain membership in a hereditary society such as the Daughters of the American Revolution (DAR), Colonial Dames, Sons of the American Revolution (SAR), the Huguenot Society, and dozens more; to prove a will or deed to establish an inheritance; to discover genetic factors for medical reasons—and geneticists usually want at least three generations on both sides of the family; to complete a family tree for personal satisfaction; to locate birth parents if adopted; or any other multitude of reasons.

Many patrons are researching their families in hopes of finding a royal ancestor and locating a coat of arms. Be aware that coats of arms were given to one person, not a family (heraldry is discussed later in this section).

There are other patrons searching for records as well as genealogists: lawyers attempting to trace beneficiaries under a will; medical researchers investigating a hereditary disease; social historians identifying factors of migration, marrying age, causes of death, economic factors, and many other reasons; owners of homes trying to trace their homes' history; Salvation Army officers trying to trace living missing persons; and Boy Scouts working on the genealogy merit badge. None of these latter patrons can be called genealogists per se, but they use many of the same records, and it is important to know what the patron is searching for and why.

Check to see what other records the patron has used—there is no use showing them materials already searched. Understand that many genealogists, especially older persons, lack training in library use and research methods. This is especially true with use of online catalogs, CD-ROM indexes, and abstracts. Most patrons will catch on fairly quickly if shown use with patience and understanding. (Genealogy patrons are very enthusiastic and driven!) Know how to use your card catalog effectively and what subject headings can prove the most fruitful to answer a question. Use care in questioning the patron. Try to avoid the "Have you checked the card catalog?" query. Do not assume the patron knows what one is, let alone how to use it, especially the online version. Be familiar with the ins and outs of interlibrary loan (ILL), and which libraries are more prone to loan their materials. No use in making recommendations to use ILL if it only leads to a dead end for the patron. Check to see if the patron has used other libraries, repositories, and especially the Mormon Family History Centers. Find out the results of their work there. If patrons are beginners, try to steer them to the Mormon Family History Centers as the place to begin their work. In addition to its main records depository, the Family History Library of the Church of Jesus Christ of Latter-day Saints, in Salt Lake City, Utah (see section 10), the church has Mormon Family History Centers throughout the world. You do not have to belong to the church to use the records, but open hours and space are limited, so be sure and phone ahead before going.

Avoid the impression you are the patron's private researcher instead of the *guide* trained to help all patrons do their own research. The idea is not to examine the patron's entire lineage, but to look for dates and places that will alert you to what you may have in your collection.

LOCAL HISTORY

I've mentioned local history several times. There is a very close relationship between genealogy and local history. In local history one can find the extras that flesh out a family and have meaning for who our ancestors were and what they did. An excellent book that can help understand this is David E. Kyvig's *Nearby History: Exploring the Past Around You* (Nashville, Tenn.: American Association for State and Local History, 1982). The American Association for State and Local History is very active in local history and has been for years. The association publishes *History News Magazine* as well as technical leaflets on various subjects, such as local history manuscripts; sources, uses, and preservation; tape recording local history; indexing local newspapers; and using memoirs to write local history. Their address is 530 Church Street, Suite 600, Nashville, TN 37219-2325; (615) 255-2971. They also have a web site, http://www.AASLh.org.

Check with the local history section of your library to see what programs you might put on together using all your resources. Contact the local or county historical society to see if you could have a combined meeting to investigate holdings and how one could complement the other.

The American Library Association (ALA), the National Genealogical Society, and the Federation of Genealogical Societies have seen the need to help librarians cope with the surge of genealogy patrons. The ALA has offered preconferences on reference service for genealogists, a minicourse for librarians, at several of its annual conferences. The two genealogical societies have offered several sessions for librarians at their annual conferences for the past couple of years. Any of these could provide insight and help for any librarian dealing with genealogy. Try to attend one of these conferences if at all possible, especially if it is held in your area. Check out your state genealogical society to see if they offer this type of program and try to attend. The national societies hold their annual conferences around the country, as does the ALA, and state societies move around their respective states.

CHILDREN AND GENEALOGY

Another trend forming is in the upper-elementary schools, middle schools, and high schools, with teachers introducing students to history through genealogy. Several gifted-student classes have had day trips to public and genealogy libraries to acquaint students with the basics of charts, what type of material is out there for them to use, and even a little on how to use it.

Books for Children

Several books are of great use for students of this age group, for example, Susan Provost Beller's *Roots for Kids: A Genealogy Guide for Young People* (Baltimore, Md.: Genealogical Publishing Co., 1997). Beller is a teacher, and she wrote this book with the aid of her students, among others. It covers such topics as "You and Your Family," "Questions to Ask," and "Putting It All Together," to mention a few items from the table of contents. If you are in a public library or any library that has a children's book collection, this would be a very good acquisition for your library. The second book I recommend is David Weitzman's *My Backyard History Book,* illustrated by James Robertson (Boston: Little, Brown and Co., 1975). It is part of the Brown Paper School series, written for both children and grown-ups. It covers such topics as getting a line on your past, a family map, how families come in all shapes and sizes, history at the cemetery, and so on. The illustrations are designed to appeal to children, and they are excellent. Another book is Catherine Bruzzone's *My Family Tree Book* (Nashville, Tenn.: Ideals Children's Books, 1991). This activity book for children will also teach them about creating a family tree, and it encourages the parents to become involved as well. Along this line is Dorling Kindersley's *Family History Activity Pack* (New York: Dorling Kindersley, 1996). For ages five and up, the kit includes a pocket camera, stickers, a record book, "past and present" playing cards, tips for starting a family photograph album, and much more. This would be ideal for the elementary-school and middle-school age groups. Something that can include the grandparents is George Allerton's *A Gift from Grandma* (Orefield, Pa.: Associated Specialities, 1990). This book has Grandma and other relatives tell the story of their families, with charts for the grandchildren to fill in the current family. Another book for children is Catherine Zahn's *All About My Family* (Arlington, Va.: National Genealogical Society, 1997). This publication focuses on the lower grades, kindergarten through third grade. The blurb for the book says it contains everything the teacher (or children's librarian) needs to know to introduce family concepts and extended family. It also uses geography, math, and art concepts to strengthen these skills for this age level as well as to develop some organizational skills.

Library Services for Children

Work with the children's librarian and have miniworkshops focusing on these books for the children. If you notice children coming into the library and asking for help in this area, ask for the name of the teacher and the school. Contact the teacher and county school board to determine exactly what the assignment is. The school board can determine if the program is countywide. If so, it might be possible to work with all the teachers to stagger the assignments around the county and not have the students descend on the county libraries at the same time. Invite teachers to your library to show what holdings are available for the various age groups of students. Make them aware of space limitations, number of copying machines, microfilm readers, computers for public use, the condition of the material, and what can and can not be heavily used. Many of the local materials may be of the vertical-file genre and can not stand heavy use without destroying the material entirely. Encourage teachers to stagger their assignments so all the teachers are not assigning the work at the same time. Work with them to develop handouts for respective grade levels. Keep the teachers abreast of new holdings in this area so they can update their assignments to incorporate this material. Ask teachers to encourage parents to come with their children, especially the younger ones, and make the parents aware of some of the problems their children will face. If you have library volunteers, they could be trained to work with the children during peak hours.

In the children's section there are many avenues for research. Here will be found books on Native Americans, costumes of colonial and pre–Civil War periods, folklore, early craftspersons and tools they used, history of America or other countries, and more—in easier to understand language.

HERALDRY

Heraldry is another area of family research that might result in a variety of questions. Heraldry can fall into both science and art as well as history. The use of coats of arms started about the late 1100s with the First Crusade. With the wearing of armor and the complete covering of heads of army commanders, there was a need to identify friends versus foes. Devices were painted on shields, banners, and surcoats, which led to the formal recognition of coats of arms and ceremonial uses as well as coats of arms becoming hereditary in the noble classes. A herald was an officer whose duties included verifying peoples' right to bear arms and their genealogies. Heralds were required to know all the coats of arms in use as well as act as messengers for the king and diplomats. Later, heralds organized tournaments, and coats of arms were used in ceremonial matters of state.

Many of the people tracing their lineage today are interested in finding royal ancestors and relating to that coat of arms. Each coat of arms is inherited through the male line, and it is usually granted, registered, and recognized to one person only. Only direct descendants who have proved their lineage are eligible to inherit some form of the original heraldic emblem. Many countries have established coats of arms and have rulings for their use. In England, contact the College of Arms, Queen Victoria Street, London EC4V 4BT. The phone number is +44 171 248 2762, and the fax number is +44 171 248 6448. Their web site is http://www.kwtelecom.com/heraldry/collarms/#T2, and this site will give much more information on heraldry. The Officer in Waiting is available for consultation during the hours of 10:00 A.M. to 4:00 P.M. London time all days but holidays, and appointments can be obtained by writing to the above address. See section 7, on genealogy books, for titles in heraldry that would be good additions to your collection. Most bookstores will have a book or two with color photographs of a variety of coats of arms, and this is where the art enters the scene. You might already have a book or two of this type in the reference section. Each part of the shield has a meaning. For an eye-catching display in your library, you might draw a shield and note the different sections and what they mean. The College of Arms also has a collection of genealogies for each registered coat of arms, and if you write to the Officer in Waiting, he might be able to help you establish a connection to an ancestor.

There is an American counterpart, The American College of Heraldry, P.O. Box 1899, Little Rock, AR 72203-1899. They will design a new coat of arms for personal use as well as use by corporations, schools, colleges, cities, branches of government, and professional and fraternal organizations. They publish *The Armiger's News,* which announces these new designs after proper registration. Their web site is http://users.aol.com/ballywoodn/Acheraldry.html. This site gives all the news about the organization.

Be active in collection development in requesting material to help *you* in serving these patrons. Keep your collection up-to-date and make sure any how-to books include the latest in computer use for genealogy, with updated sources. Keep one how-to book at the reference desk, such as Ralph Crandall's *Shaking Your Family Tree* (Camden, Maine: Yankee Books, 1988). It is easy to read and gives lots of good tips. You might also suggest one for the children's reference desk to have handy for use there as well.

You will no doubt have some people come in looking for their family coats of arms. As stated before, there is no such thing. You may have seen ads offering family coats of arms for sale on carts in your local shopping mall. It is a waste of money unless you just want one for its artistic work. These types of works are no more than improper and illegitimate uses of the designs. Although there are no federal or state laws governing this abuse of coats of arms, it is still unethical to use any of these that are legitimately assigned to other people.

PERIODICALS

Another good area to find information on genealogy is in periodicals—and not necessarily genealogy periodicals. *Time, Newsweek,* and *American Heritage,* among others, have all had articles on family history at one time or another. Many library journals have published articles on libraries and genealogy patrons. *Library Literature* indexes these articles and is online as well; or you can use OCLC's FirstSearch to help locate them. Here are just a few of the titles as a start.

> *Library Trends* (v. 32, summer 1983) devoted the entire issue to genealogy and libraries.
> *Library Journal* (v. 117, no. 18, November 1992, pp. 51–55), "Branching Out into Genealogy," by Judith P. Reid
> *Reference Librarian* (no. 22, 1988, pp. 283–95), "Instruction for Genealogists in the Public Library," by Craig R. Amason
> *RQ* (v. 23, no. 2, winter 1983) devoted a large part of this issue to helping the librarian help patrons.

Many other journals have articles bearing on this topic as well, much too numerous to list here. Some of these journals are *Current Trends in Reference*

Service, New Jersey Libraries, Texas Libraries, Show-Me Libraries, Mississippi Libraries, Judaica Librarianship, Bookmark, Reference Service Review, and *Journal of Academic Librarianship.* They cover such topics as basic genealogy collection for public libraries, genealogy in the academic library, reference works for genealogists, how to use the law library in interpreting the laws of our ancestors, and how to handle the genealogical patron, among others. These articles started to appear around 1976 and have been fairly frequent since. Be sure to check your indexes for more on this subject. Note others you find here for ready reference.

SECTION 3

Checklist of Genealogical Sources and Abbreviations Used in Genealogy

This section gives a variety of records that are available for genealogists to use in their search for their family history and abbreviations for words used in genealogical research. As you can see, some of these sources are located in the home, and that is logically where genealogical research should begin. These records are common to us all, and we should know where our own records are and if they are properly housed for ready access. Are they properly safeguarded against fire, hurricanes, tornadoes, water damage, or insects? These records are no less important than the records of our ancestors. Gather your own records and place them in a scrapbook with archival-quality paper. You will find many hours of pleasure reviewing your own life and the memories this will bring.

HOME SOURCES

General   Most of these will need no explanation.

Account books   Photograph albums
Baby books   Scrapbooks
Citizenship papers   Family Bibles
Employment records   Heirlooms—get their history
Farm records   Letters
Health or medical records   Memorial cards
Journals and diaries   Oral traditions
Military files, medals, etc.   Social Security cards
School records, such as yearbooks,
   diplomas, report cards, etc.

Certificates   Be sure to check both sides, especially of marriage records, for the witnesses and the attendees of the ceremony. They could be family members and names for further research and for rounding out a family group sheet.

Birth	Marriage
Death	Adoption
Baptism	Confirmation
Graduation	Fraktur—Moravian or German
Manumission—freedom granted to slaves	form for religious certificates
	Annulment
Divorce	

Probate Records

Be sure to check witnesses to wills, as the names might be those of relatives.

Wills	Administrations
Inventories	Bonds
Settlements	Guardianships

Cemetery Records

Sexton records identify the exact location of the grave. If it is a family plot, record all the names, as only family members can be buried in the plot. These records can also tell who is responsible for payment for and upkeep of the plot, another possible relative.

Sexton records	Monuments, tombstones
Plats	Perpetual care
Memorials	Gifts
Deeds	

Mortuary Records

Burial registers	Funeral cards
Funeral books	

Military Records

Service files	Pensions
Bounty awards	Discharge papers
Muster rolls	

Institutional Records

Contributions to and memberships in various societies can tell social activity and give an insight into the whole picture of the ancestor.

Charities	Hospitals
Convents	Seminaries
Libraries	Historical societies
Mission societies	Orphanages
Reunion registries	Masonic membership
Other fraternal organization records	

Employment Records

Such records offer a possible lead to the ancestor's occupation and leads to other work-related organizations (e.g., union membership).

Indentures	Licenses
Apprenticeships	Service awards
Pensions	Account books
Personnel files	

Tax Records

Tax records can give the prosperity or lack thereof of an ancestor.

Poll tax	Personal property
School tax	Poor law records
Real estate tax	Income tax forms

Immigrant Records

These can lead to the ancestral homeland.

Passenger lists	Passports
Alien registration cards	Oaths of allegiance
Naturalization records	Citizenship papers
Customs records	Immigrant aid societies
Ships' logbooks	Change-of-name papers
Register of voters	

Church Records

Birth	Marriage
Baptism	Christening
Ordination	Banns
Annulment	Removals
Subscription lists	Ministers' records
Disciplinary proceedings	Death
Burial	

Land Records   Deeds   Mortgages
                    Grantee index   Grantor index
                    Patents, grants   Surveys

ABBREVIATIONS

b	born	gp	grandparents
bap	baptised	h	husband
bmd	birth, marriage, death	IRC	International Reply Coupon
bur	buried		
bro	brother	liv	living
c/ca	about, used with dates	m	married
cem	cemetery	ml	mother-in-law
cen	census	mo	mother
cert	certificate	na	naturalized
ch	child	n.d.	no date
chris	christened	P	parents
Co	County	par	parish
CW	Civil War	pro	probate
d	died	PRO	Public Record Office, England and Wales
dau	daughter		
dec/d	deceased	prov	province
dist	district	res	resided
div	divorced	R.I.P.	rest in peace
dob	date of birth	RW	Revolutionary War
dod	date of death	SASE	self-addressed, stamped envelope
d.s.p.	died without issue		
ed	enumeration district, used in census	sis	sister
		sl	son-in-law
exec	executor	s/o	son of
f	father	SRO	Scottish Record Office
fam	family/ies	Twp	township
g	great	vr	vital records
gf	grandfather	w	wife
ggf	great grandfather	wid	widow
gm	grandmother		

Add others here as found.

SECTION 4 ❧

Census Records and Forms, 1800–1920

The U.S. federal census has been taken every ten years since 1790. Its purpose originally was to allocate taxes and representation in Congress among the several states according to their populations.

This group of records is probably the most used group of records by genealogists. Finding an ancestor in a census will establish that person in place and time. The first censuses, from 1790 to 1840, enumerated only the head of the household, with other members of the household indicated in respective sex and age groups only by check marks. The U.S. Department Of Commerce and Labor Bureau of the Census has published *Heads of Families at the First Census of the United States Taken in the Year 1790* (Washington, D.C.: GPO, 1908). The following states' records have been printed in book form: Connecticut, Maine, Maryland, Massachusetts, Hew Hampshire, New York, North Carolina, Pennsylvania, Rhode Island, South Carolina, Vermont, and Virginia. The records for Delaware, Georgia, Kentucky, New Jersey, and Tennessee were destroyed.

Many tax lists and militia lists have been published, and these can be used in place of the destroyed schedules. Check published lists of books and periodical indexes for these, especially in the area of interest. There was little uniformity in the method of recording the first few census schedules. The early census takers used whatever paper was available. The census forms now printed for those years were taken from lists of information wanted. In 1830 the government printed the first formal forms for use by all census takers. This served the purpose of Congress for a few years, but as time went on, everyone realized more information was needed.

Then in 1850 every member of the household was recorded in the census, a true enumeration of the population. Although the previous returns could have some genealogical value for researchers, it is these later schedules that are of great importance. Schedule forms from 1800 to 1920 (except for 1890) are included so you can see how the additional information required each year would be of value. See appendixes 5 through 14.

Note that the 1920 form is the latest included. A seventy-two-year moratorium precludes releasing census information prior to that date to protect the privacy of the living. The release of the 1930 census returns, therefore, will take place in the year 2002. The National Archives has microfilmed all these schedules, and they are available at the archives and branches as well as all the Mormon Family History Centers. You do not have to belong to the church to use their records, and you are most welcome there. The centers are staffed by volunteers, and open hours are limited so check before going. Many large libraries and genealogical centers also have copies of some of the films as well as printed indexes for the 1850–1890 years.

There were also special census schedules taken from 1850 to 1880. They detailed manufacturing, agriculture, industry, and mortality. Also, many states scheduled censuses in the five-year periods between the federal census (e.g., 1885). There were also census schedules for the territories out West before they became states. The 1890 census was pretty much destroyed by fire and is not available for researching except for a few states. There was also a special census of the Union Civil War Veterans and veterans' widows taken in 1890, and part of this survived that fire.

SOUNDEX

For the 1880, 1900, 1910, and 1920 years, a special index was created for these schedules called Soundex. This system grouped all surnames by sound. The 1880 Soundex included only those families with children under ten years of age, so you would have to look at the entire census, reel by reel, if a name is not included in the Soundex. Names are coded by writing the first letter of the surname and then using numbers for the remaining letters. Vowels, *y*, *w*, and *h* are crossed out of the name. Thus, *Moore* would be *M*, cross out the two *o*s, change the *r* to 6, and cross out the *e*, and you have M 600. The surname must be an initial letter and three numbers—no more, no less. The table that governs this follows:

1 = b, p, f, v
2 = c, s, k, g, j, q, x, z
3 = d, t
4 = l
5 = m, n
6 = r
Other examples: Lee   = L 000
                Smith   = S 530
                Gardiner = G 635

Double consonants in a name (such as the double *o* in the name Moore) are given one number. See Bradley Steuart's *Soundex Reference Guide* (Bountiful, Utah: Precision Indexing, 1990) for a fuller explanation of this system as well as a listing of hundreds of names with their codes.

USING CENSUS RECORDS

To use the census, you must know the county of the state or the ward in the larger cities such as New York. Counties changed boundaries as states grew, so it can sometimes be problematic locating the ancestor from one census year to another. See William Thorndale and William Dollarhide's *Map Guide to the U.S. Federal Censuses, 1790–1920* (Baltimore, Md.: Genealogical Publishing Co., 1987), which gives not only all these changes in map form for each of the census years, but also a bit of the history of the census taking, with all kinds of hints on using the census itself.

Some cautions in using the census must be considered. The handwriting, for one thing, can be very confusing. Some entries are very clear, but others need a lot of guessing to decipher. Moreover, we are not sure just who gave the information. It could be the family themselves, a neighbor, a child, or the census taker, who found an empty house the first time he or she came by and might have taken a guess if he or she knew the family. Check out Richard H. Saldana, ed., *A Practical Guide to the "MISTEAKS" Made in Census Indexes* (Bountiful, Utah: Precision Indexing, 1987) for further insight on this topic.

When using the census schedules, be sure to record all information, starting with the top of the page: state, county, township or other county division, ward of a city, enumeration district, date the census was taken, name of the census taker, street name, house number, family number, and so forth. Be sure to scan up and down the page where your family is located to note all those who are neighbors. A census taker usually worked one side of the street, then crossed over and did the other side; so it is important to note families on both sides of the street. They might also be family or in-laws. In spite of these limitations, the census enumeration schedules are a vital part of genealogical research. By locating a person in the census, you can find names of all persons in that household, relationship to head of household, or children you might not have known existed. Check to see if any holdings of the enumerated census (from 1850 on) are available in your area, and make note of them for your patrons. From 1790 to 1840, only the head of household was enumerated, or named. From 1850 on, all persons living at that address—whether it was a house, boardinghouse, nunnery, house of prostitution, and so forth—had to be named. This is what is referred to as "the enumerated census." Many genealogical societies have some reels of the census, usually of their state or of the area, such as the Southeast, New England, and so forth.

OTHER CENSUSES

One of the first censuses taken was in England in 1086, after the conquest by William the Conqueror in 1066. He wanted to know the extent of the country he had just conquered. This is called the *Domesday Book.* We will not discuss this further here, but check *Encyclopedia Britannica* for details of this work.

The first modern-day census in England and Wales took place in 1801, and like the early censuses in the United States, it does not give much genealogical information. The census in England took place every ten years, as it has in the United States, though one year later. The first census to give more information was in 1841, when all persons in the household were named. Even so, it only gave the name, sex, occupation, and whether they were born in the same county. The 1851 English census is of much more value for genealogists, with a great deal of valuable information to be found. These census records are also available for viewing in the Mormon Family History Centers, as are Canada's records. There is a 100-year privacy rule in the United Kingdom, and the latest census available for study is for 1891.

There was also an Ecclesiastical Census of 1851. All denominations were expected to take a census of places of worship. Information on this census included the date of consecration or erection, totals in attendance at the various services on March 1851, and average attendances for the previous year. These records are housed in the Public Record Office (PRO). The address is Ruskin Avenue, Kew, Richmond, Surrey, TW9 4DU, United Kingdom, and the web site is http://www.pro.gov.uk. The PRO is the repository of the national archives for the United Kingdom, and the records span from the eleventh century to the present. Though not of much value for names, they can be of value in tracing the churches that existed in a particular district. That could give clues as to what church your ancestor might have attended at that particular time as well as when these houses of worship were erected. Using this census, you can check the parish registers kept by the pastors and perhaps find the names and relationships you are searching.

Other Genealogical Records: Vital Records, Passenger Lists, Land Records, and Wills and Probate

VITAL RECORDS

What do we mean by vital records? Birth, marriage, and death records have long been considered vital records. Today we might also add adoption and dissolution or divorce records, though adoption and divorce are usually associated more with court records and will not be discussed here. Vital records are kept basically on four levels: (1) local and city level, common on the East Coast of the United States; (2) county; (3) state; and (4) federal, for births on overseas military bases, foreign service, and reservations.

It is also necessary to know a little of the history of recording these events. Most of the early settlers of the United States came from England, and they brought with them the systems they knew there. After the break with the Catholic Church in the 1500s and early 1600s, parish ministers were required to keep a record of all christenings, marriages, and burials in their parishes. Parish registers are where you must do research in the United Kingdom prior to 1837, when the government assumed the task of recording these events. However, do not ask for *vital records* in the United Kingdom, as you will not be understood. There, vital records are the measurements of the chest, waist, and hips. You have to ask for *civil registration records* if you hope to continue your research there. Civil registration records of birth, marriage, death, and adoption certificates in England are located in the Office for National Statistics at the Family Records Centre, 1 Myddelton Street, London, England, EC1R 1UW. For more information, go to the web site: http://www.pro.gov.uk/readers/genealogists/certificates.htm.

The first known law in the colonies was passed in 1632 by the Grand Assembly of Virginia. All residents of Virginia were required to register births, deaths, and other events with the Church of England, regardless of their religious affiliation. The Mormon Church has microfilmed most of these parish registers, and they are available in the Mormon Family History Centers. In 1639 the Massachusetts Bay Colony passed a law that town clerks record dates of births, marriages, and deaths, rather than christenings and burials. For births, they usually give the name of the child and of the parents. Thus, if you have gotten back that far in your research, these are the records you need to consult rather than state records. Many genealogical and historical societies have abstracted and published these records in their journals as well as books. One example of this is Jane Fletcher Fiske and Margaret D. Costello, eds., *Vital Records of Swansea, Massachusetts to 1850,* transcribed by H. L. Peter Rounds (Boston: New England Historic Genealogical Society, 1992). Almost all the vital records of Massachusetts have now been printed in book form.

Starting in the late 1800s, states passed laws requiring registry of births, marriages, and deaths with the necessary agencies. States vary in the years this started, the agencies where these records are housed, and the years when the law was enforced. Check Thomas Jay Kemp's *International Vital Records Handbook* (Baltimore, Md.: Genealogical Publishing Co., 1990). This book includes copies of the necessary forms required to send for these certificates as well as the agencies where to send the form, what records are available where, and the cost (the cost was as of 1990, when the book was printed, and could vary at the present time).

When writing for a copy of a record, be sure to request a certified copy of the record to ensure getting all the information on the record. If you are unsure of the exact date, request a ten-year spread of dates—five years on either side of the suspected one. Your chances of positive results are much better. You should also send the person's age, spouse, parents, location of town or city, county, and state. However, do not send your entire genealogy; clerks do not have the time to read it to find out what you are actually requesting.

These are the basic records you must have for proper documentation of the genealogy.

Birth Records

What type of information can you expect to find? Birth records were usually required after 1880, depending on the state, and could be recorded in the city or county clerk's office. A copy was also required to be sent to the state. Usually found on this type of record is the name and sex of the baby, father's and mother's names, and the place of birth. In later years you can also find ages of father and mother, number of births of mother, number of live births of mother, possible birthplaces of mother and father, name of the doctor who delivered the baby, name of hospital if it occurred there, and the residence of the parents.

If you can not find a birth recorded in the earlier years, it could mean a home birth and the parents never got around to registering the fact or the parents may have lived on a farm a long way from the town and might possibly have registered the birth in a church rather than the courthouse. There might also be a delayed birth certificate long after the fact if there were bona fide witnesses to the birth. Many people registering for Social Security in the 1930s and 1940s only then realized they had no birth certificate and had to file for delayed ones at that time.

Another avenue to explore is midwives' records. Most midwives kept a record of their deliveries, listing date, name of the baby, name of the father, and how much they were paid. These can be found in various society journals or special publications.

Marriage Records

Counties started requiring marriage records or documents because officials found records necessary to ensure land ownership transfer. Historically, there was also something called *common-law marriage*. In rural towns and villages that relied on a traveling minister who might come only once a year, local couples made their intentions known in town and even lived together until the proper authority made his rounds. If a child was born before this happened, they were considered married, so there might be no marriage record at all. In later years and to date, blood tests were required for issuance of a marriage license.

What can you expect to find in marriage records? Names of the bride and groom, date of ceremony, place. They can also contain the ages of the bride and groom, names and addresses of parents of each, name of the minister and church where the ceremony was performed, and witnesses listed, who could also be relatives. Be sure to check the back of the certificate for these names. Also check for banns, which were announced in church for the three weeks prior to the ceremony, especially in the Church of England (Episcopalian) and the Catholic Church. Furthermore, applications for a license can also give a lot of information on the bride and groom. Newspapers are also a good source for recording the ceremony. Think of today's newspapers and the accounts of marriages and what information they can give as well as pictures of the happy couple. Small-town newspapers would give a fuller account of the ceremony, including some guests' names, possible place of reception, and so forth.

Death Records

Death records were also required by the states at varying time periods. They were very important for the transfer of land and wealth to the next of kin.

What information can we find here? The death certificate can contain the name of the deceased, date of death, place of death, age at death, and, as time went on, can also have the birth date, name of spouse, whether widow or widower, name of parents, place of burial, date of burial, cause of death (important in tracing genetic diseases), name of physician at death, length of illness, address of deceased, and who gave the information. Depending upon this last item, you must use caution when accepting the information as absolutely true. This is a time of great stress for the family. The spouse might be too grief stricken to give the information or even remember it accurately. It could come from a child, who may or may not know the exact information; or from a neighbor and friend who only guesses at the dates and names; or it could be left blank. The doctors' statements are usually considered primary information, as presumably they should know their patients by name, the cause of death, and the date.

When you know a death date, check the local newspaper for an obituary. The further back you go in time, the quicker the burial, usually one to two days after death. If death occurred in a smaller town and the deceased was a resident there for a time, there would be an obituary that could highlight much family information. Also check for probate records or check the newspaper again for a reading of the will. Church records are also likely to have a death recorded and could relate where the burial took place. Check funeral-home records to see if any existed for the time period. If the funeral home is no longer in existence, try the local historical society or check with another funeral home for information as to where it moved or if it was taken over by another parlor. If so, check with them as to previous records. See *National Directory of Morticians, the Red Book* (Chagrin Falls, Ohio: National Directory of Morticians, annual); and Deborah M. Burek, ed., *Cemeteries of the U.S.: A Guide to Contact Information for U.S. Cemeteries and Their Records* (Washington, D.C.: Gale Research, 1994).

Before visiting a cemetery, check with the sexton's or church office. Here you could receive a map of the cemetery, the exact location of the grave, and information on whether it is a family plot. If it is a family plot, note who else is buried there, as only family members can be buried in a family plot. If you are having trouble finding birth and marriage records, try working backward and start with a death certificate or an obituary. As mentioned, it could give at least a general place of birth, former residence, parents' names, and location of burial. Also check in the area of last residence known to you and work from there.

PASSENGER LISTS

Most Americans have immigrant ancestors, whether they arrived in the 1600s or any time later. The reasons for leaving their homelands were varied, from religious persecution, war, famine, striving for a better life, or hoping to own some land. Locating these immigrant ancestors can be a challenge. Closely tied with passenger lists are immigration and naturalization papers. Sometimes one has to find the latter to locate the former. The National Archives has most of the American passenger lists available in the United States, dating from about 1820 to 1945. There are three types: customs passenger lists, immigration passenger lists, and customs lists of aliens. Most of these are limited in port and time frame. Fortunately for us, various people have attempted to help us out by publishing lists exactly as they have been found. Check Ira A. Glazier and Michael H. Tepper, eds., *The Famine Immigrants: Lists of Irish Immigrants Arriving at the Port of New York, 1846–1851*, 7 vols. (Baltimore, Md.: Genealogical Publishing Co., 1983–1986); and Ira A. Glazier and P. William Filby, eds., *Germans to America: Lists of Passengers Arriving at U.S. Ports, 1850–1893* (Wilmington, Del.: Scholarly Resources, 1988–). The latter is an ongoing series, with seven volumes published so far. These are not the only two, so check Marian Hoffman, ed., *Genealogical and Local History Books in Print*, 5th ed., 5 vols. (Baltimore, Md.: Genealogical Publishing Co., 1997), to find others. Probably the largest collection of passenger records in print is a work by P. William Filby, *Passenger and Immigration Lists Index* (Detroit, Mich.: Gale Research, 1981), which has had a supplement published every year since 1981. The entries are listed by name followed by a source number. The source entries are in the front of each volume and will relate where the information was located. From that, you can use interlibrary loan (ILL) or go to a Mormon Family History Center or a local genealogy library if one is in your area.

In 1819 Congress passed laws requiring ship captains to file a list of all passengers and crew at the port of arrival. This also included any passengers who died or were born on the crossing. These lists are very helpful as they list every member of the family, the date and port of embarkation, the name of the ship, date of arrival, sex of the passengers, sometimes occupation, and usually the name of the country where they intended to settle. These reports were then collected by the U.S. Customs Service and eventually found their way to the National Archives, where they have been microfilmed. By the late 1890s printed forms were introduced and included more information on the passengers. They included the names of all American citizens on board as well. From personal experience, it is indeed helpful to know the approximate date of arrival, especially at the Port of New York. The lists for New York are indexed only from 1820 to 1846 and from 1897 to 1948. The in-between period requires checking each reel.

There are other ways to try and locate an immigrant. Try the census records. If the person is not on the 1870 census but is listed on the 1880 census, that will narrow your search by several years. Check the birth of the children to see where they were born, and if one is born in another country and one in the United States, you have narrowed the time frame even more. You can then go to the passenger lists for a search. The National Archives publication *Immigrant Passenger Arrivals: A Select Catalog of National Archives Microfilm Publications* (Washington, D.C.: National Archives Trust Fund Board, 1983) lists the microfilms by port and reel number.

If your immigrant ancestor arrived at the Port of New York between January 1892 and November 1954, he or she probably came through Ellis Island. Not only were the passenger arrival records created here, but there were also other records created as well. As immigrants passed through the center, they created records from the customs, immigration, and health officials. There has been a restoration of Ellis Island, and a museum is now open to the public with scenes depicting the activities of arrival there. In the future, officials hope to have a computer program listing all the passenger arrival lists available for searching. You can write to Ellis Island Immigration Museum, Statue of Liberty National Monument, Liberty Island, New York, NY, 10004. Or call (212) 363-5804 for the museum and (212) 363-6681 for the library. The web site, http://www.wallofhonor.com, allows you to view the American Immigrant Wall of Honor, where you can see a registered family name or register your family name using an electronic form. Another tip is to check the local newspapers in the port areas as each newspaper usually has a listing of what ships arrived each day, where they came from, and whether they carried passengers. That could help your search even more.

LAND RECORDS

Land records are some of the oldest forms of records that genealogists can use. They record when a person lived in a certain place and time and are of great importance in establishing our heritage. The English brought their laws governing land transactions to the colonies with them as well as land grants from the king to individuals. Companies were formed in England that sold rights to property in the colonies, and the wording caused difficulties as many of the rights stated that this land extended from sea to sea. As the settlers moved west, contentions over parcels of land were created due to this wording, creating marvelous court records. Eventually the federal government stepped in, and many lands became part of the public domain. Such land was surveyed and later sold at auction or given to veterans of the Revolutionary War and the War of 1812.

There are two types of lands: states lands and federal lands. *State lands* were those that the states originally controlled and dispersed and were mainly those of the original thirteen colonies, Hawaii, Texas, Kentucky, Tennessee, and West Virginia. These lands are measured by metes and bounds and had been in place during the colonial period and in individual hands by the time the U.S. federal government came into being. *Federal lands* came into being in 1785 and were created to raise revenue, to grant land as rewards to soldiers, and to encourage westward migration. These lands were based on a *meridian,* divided into tracts, and then laid out in townships and ranges. Each township is in a six-mile square, with ranges running north and south, six miles apart. Working with these systems of land can be very complicated and needs a lot more detailed study than can be expressed here. See appendix 15. A publication that gives all the details of how to work with land records is E. Wade Hone's *Land and Property Research in the United States* (Salt Lake City, Utah: Ancestry, 1997).

Land was one of the prime reasons immigrants came to the United States, outside of religious persecution. Land was plentiful and cheap and many could afford to purchase it when this was impossible in their country of origin. Land records were the first records to be re-created when a courthouse burned. They also were closely related in importance to marriage records, as wives had dower rights. These rights entitled a wife to one-third of the deceased husband's estate, and so her name was often mentioned in the husband's will. This system was brought from England and continues in some states today. A wife could also be mentioned if she received land as heir of her father, thus giving her maiden name. She could not own the land in her own right, so it passed to her husband, and this also could be mentioned in the transfer of this land to the husband, again giving her maiden name and the name of her father. Check Marylynn Salmon's *Women and the Law of Property in Early America* (Chapel Hill: University of North Carolina Press, 1986), which gives a good perspective of dower rights in the various colonies.

Many other records were created in the process of acquiring land. One had to file an application; next, the land had to be surveyed; it was then recorded in a tract book and a final certificate was issued. There are also the Military Bounty land warrants, homestead records, applications for mines and timberlands, and more. The Bureau of Land Management is the overall governing agency for federal lands, and its address is Bureau of Land Management, Eastern States Office, 7450 Boston Boulevard, Springfield, VA 22153. There are bureau offices in many states as well. Check your phone book under the federal government section, and add that information here. The bureau is also creating an online index for federal land records under its jurisdiction. There eventually will be a CD-ROM for each of the completed states. The various branches of the National Archives also have copies of this CD-ROM for the various states they cover. Section 14, on the National Archives, lists addresses of each branch and what states are covered in their holdings. If you own property, check your own land deed and note the information available there. From this, you can see what our ancestors' deeds can impart for the family historian.

Other publications that deal with land records are Clifford Neal Smith, *Federal Land Series: A Calendar of Archival Materials of the Land Patents Issued by the*

United States Government with Subject, Tract, and Name Indexes, 5 vols. (Chicago: American Library Association, 1971–1986); E. Kay Kirkham, *The Land Records of America and Their Genealogical Value* (Salt Lake City, Utah: Deseret Book Co., 1964); and Charles Butler Barr, *Townships and Legal Descriptions of Land,* 2d ed. (Independence, Miss.: C. B. Barr, 1992). This gives a few titles, and E. Wade Hone has an excellent bibliography in his book *Land and Property Research in the United States* (Salt Lake City, Utah: Ancestry, Inc., 1997). Also check out such titles as Arlene Eakle and Johni Cerny, *The Source: A Guidebook of American Genealogy* (Salt Lake City, Utah: Ancestry, 1996); Val D. Greenwood, *The Researcher's Guide to American Genealogy,* 2d ed. (Baltimore, Md.: Genealogical Publishing Co., 1990); or any good how-to book for more information. James W. Oberly's *Sixty Million Acres: American Veterans and the Public Lands before the Civil War* (Kent, Ohio: Kent State University Press, 1990) gives an excellent account of the military bounty lands.

WILLS AND PROBATE

Wills and the probate process are very fruitful areas of research for genealogists. Today we have printed forms for use when drawing up a will. Much of the legal terminology is already printed and just the details of the disposal of the property are added. The English brought to the United States their laws determining disposal of property but with some differences. In England the probate process was performed by the Church of England in the Ecclesiastical Courts. As the colonies did not have this procedure, each colony took on the function and determined its own laws. Thus, the United States has a variety of laws, offices, and processes to determine the disposition of property on the death of a person.

When a person dies, various laws of the state of residence determine how the estate is handled, especially if there is no will and there are minor children. In this case, the person with no will is said to die intestate. According to the laws of the state, the property is divided among the surviving relatives, and guardians are appointed for the minor children. This will involve additional records to be searched, such as guardianships and court cases.

A will is nothing more than a legal document disposing of the real and personal property of a person (the testator) according to his or her wishes. The will becomes effective upon the death of the testator and not before. Some wills are very long, others are short, and sometimes there is humor in the document. See "To My Wife, I Leave Her Lover," by Joe McCarthy, *This Week Magazine* (September 26, 1965), p. 12.

More than one will can be written, but "the last will and testament" is the one that will be executed and take precedence over all previous wills. A codicil can be attached to a will if it is properly executed and filed with the will. There is a legal process involved, which is not considered here. Terminology in the will can be explained by looking in *Black's Law Dictionary with Pronunciations,* 6th ed. (St. Paul, Minn.: West Publishing Co., 1990), which explains all the older legal terms. Most libraries will have a copy of this in the reference section. You can add the call number here for easy reference.

With this legal process of filing probate of a will, many more records will be created, and all should be examined. There can be an inventory of the estate, listing all the holdings of the deceased. This can give an insight into the economic standing of the person. It will also give a monetary value of the estate and list all debts owed and debts owed in return and whether those debts were collected. These could include the amount paid to the grave digger, giving an approximate date of death if not already known; fees paid to the doctor for the last illness; amounts paid to relatives; names of persons land was purchased from and who inherited the land; and so forth.

Slaves could also be listed by name with their dispositions and whether they were kept in the family or sold. Usually the will names all the children, including the married names of the females, but if any children received their inheritances previously, they might not be mentioned here. Unfortunately, sometimes the phrase "my wife" is used, with no name listed; or the phrase "all my children" is used, again with no names. As with other compiled indexes and abstracts, there can be errors in the transcription caused by misinterpreting the handwriting, copying in haste, and careless copying by the person doing the abstracting. If a will seems of interest to you, write to the county courthouse or the state archives for a copy of the will and all other documents involved, such as inventories, estate papers, executor's records, and any sales receipts. All could give much insight to the way your ancestor lived and worked.

Many societies, the Daughters of the American Revolution (DAR), and other organizations have been busy abstracting some of these older wills. Check *Genealogical and Local History Books in Print*, 5th ed. (Baltimore, Md.: Genealogical Publishing Co., 1997) for listings in your area. New Jersey has reprinted a new series of abstracts from its archives: *Calendar of New Jersey Wills and Administrations Covering the Years 1670–1780*, 2 vols. (Westminster, Md.: Family Line Publications, 1997). This series has been published by Heritage Press and Family Line Publications in various volumes. The Tea Burning Chapter of the DAR, in Cumberland County, New Jersey, has done the abstracts from 1804 to 1855. Copies of these will abstracts by the DAR are located in the National Society Daughters of the American Revolution (DAR) Library, 1776 D Street NW, Washington, DC 20006–5392. Copies of the wills themselves are not only in the state archives, but also in the county courthouse in Cumberland County, New Jersey. Check to see what your state has done along these lines. Call the county courthouse in your county to see what the situation is in your area. Find out if the records are open to the public, what years are covered, and whether photocopying facilities are available and at what price, and add that information here.

SECTION 6

General Books Most Libraries Should Own

Many of the resources here are very common in most public and academic libraries, as are history books on a local as well as worldwide level. If the local university offers courses in women's history, public history, and social sciences, the academic library will have a greater coverage of these fields that can also be used in genealogical research. The academic library will also have a wider selection of databases online that can be searched using genealogy subject headings. Academic libraries usually have a greater run of journal titles, with more than adequate back files. Such libraries have begun to feel pressure from people coming in and wanting help in this field of study, and libraries realize their holdings are more than adequate to cover at least the basic beginnings of family history. The reference department might also have a general bibliography of sources in the library that can be used for genealogical purposes. I started one in the Florida Atlantic University Library in 1986 and have updated it every two to three years to include new material as well as online sources. If you have any of the following titles in your holdings, add call number and location next to the title for quick access.

Adoption Directory. 2d ed. Edited by Ellen Paul. Detroit, Mich.: Gale Research, 1995.

> A comprehensive guide to adoption including state statutes and public and private adoption agencies. Can give leads for the adoptee as to where to write for information. The Freedom of Information Act has opened up many records previously sealed. Provides state-by-state and country-by-country surveys of adoption agencies, foreign agencies' listings, independent adoption services and their fees, foster care, and support groups.

Albion's Seed. David Hackett Fischer. New York, Oxford University Press, 1989.

> This covers four main migrations from the British Isles: "English Puritans, 1629–1641"; "Cavaliers and Indentured Servants, 1642–1675"; "Friends' Migration, 1675–1725"; and "Flight from North Britain, 1717–1775." Excellent background reading for reasons why your ancestors

might have migrated when they did from Great Britain. It makes great reading for those who have ancestors coming during the various time periods.

American Heritage Dictionary of the English Language. Boston, Mass.: Houghton Mifflin, latest edition.

Look here for definitions of older terms and words, such as occupations, trades, and so forth. Contains short biographical data, geographical names, abbreviations, and some foreign terms as well as writing, pronunciation, and vocabulary assistance. The *Oxford English Dictionary* (OED) (Oxford: Oxford University Press, 1989) is also very valuable in this regard, as are other comprehensive dictionaries. Don't overlook some of the older editions of dictionaries, as words and their meanings change over time.

American History Sourcebook. Edited by Joel Makower. New York: Prentice Hall Press, 1988.

"A comprehensive guide to museums, libraries, archives, photo collections, historical societies, and other sources of information in U.S. history, politics, and culture," as stated on the cover. Details the types of collections housed in each entry. Very useful if a patron is planning a trip to know what resources are in the area and open for visits.

American Library Directory. 2 vols. New York: R. R. Bowker, biennial.

Alphabetical by state for the United States, provinces in Canada, and U.S. territories. Lists public, academic, and special libraries, giving all pertinent information as to address, phone number, and so forth. Be sure to check holdings entry, as that will give information on local history collections as well as denote if genealogical materials are housed there.

Biography and Genealogy Master Index. Detroit, Mich.: Gale Research, annual.

Covers more than 3,200,000 biographical sketches in more than 350 current and retrospective biographical dictionaries. Includes sources of information and a list of title codes used in locating sources. It now is on CD-ROM, which is very user friendly.

Black's Law Dictionary with Pronunciations. 6th ed. St. Paul, Minn.: West Publishing Co., 1990.

Very important when dealing with will and probate documents as well as land records. Legal terminology can be very confusing, and this work is indispensable in sorting through the meanings. Includes English terms as well. The law library is one of the oldest type of libraries in the states. Law was practiced in the colonial period, and state, territory, and federal governments passed laws. Each jurisdiction kept records of their own laws, and they are available today.

Chicago Manual of Style. Chicago: University of Chicago Press, 14th ed., 1993.

A basic "how-to" book for anyone wanting to write and publish his or her family history. Covers manuscript preparation, punctuation, documentation, parts of a book, indexing, and so forth.

CIS U.S. Serial Set Index. Washington, D.C.: Congressional Information Service, 1975–.

This is a collection of U.S. government documents compiled under the direction of Congress, dating from 1789. *Grassroots of America*, compiled by Phillip W. McMullen (Salt Lake City, Utah: Gendex Corp., 1972), is the index to the portion of the American State Papers, the earliest portion of the work. These are included in the first volumes of the index as well. The arrangement is roughly in chronological order, by Congress and session. Volume 1 begins with the first session of the fifteenth Congress. Sections 8, Public Lands, and 9, Claims, are of most interest to genealogists, as claimants usually gave information about themselves and sometimes about their families. Claims could also take many years to be resolved and could include a couple of generations as well. Also included are the official records of the War of the Rebellion; look under *rebellion* in the index. The records are on fiche.

City Directories. Variety of publishers.

Publication of city directories started in the early to mid-1800s. They cover streets in a given location; citizens are usually listed alphabetically by surname, with addresses, occupations, and businesses. Don't forget to check all the ads of businesses for additional information. They usually list all churches, schools, cemeteries, and so forth. Many public libraries collect these for their town, city, or county and keep them in the local history room. The Library of Congress has one of the largest collections of these. City directories are also available in fiche and microfilm format.

Columbia Lippincott Gazetteer of the World. New York: Columbia University Press, 1962.

As the title states, this covers the world. Gives location of many towns, cities with their counties, and places no longer in existence for one reason or another. Invaluable for all the places where our ancestors were born and possibly can't be located in any other way. Includes a bit of historical data about the place names as well.

Directory of Archives and Manuscript Repositories in the United States. Phoenix, Ariz.: Oryx Press, 1988.

Arranged alphabetically by state, then city and institution, with pertinent information (i.e., address, phone number, hours open, availability of copying facilities, types of materials solicited, and holdings). Be sure to check out the last two entries as they give a wealth of information about types of materials collected and materials owned.

Directory of Historical Organizations and Agencies in the United States and Canada. Nashville, Tenn.: American Association of State and Local History, biennial.

Lists names and addresses of societies as well as libraries and museums, with hours and publications. Most important is the section that
covers the scope of historical collections. This is an excellent way to
locate local history material needed for background of ancestors.

Directory of Special Libraries and Information Centers. Detroit, Mich.: Gale
Research, annual.

Entries include name of the institution, address, phone number, direc-
tor, subjects covered in the holdings, services such as interlibrary loan
(ILL), prices charged for photocopies, and whether open to the public.
The subject index includes headings such as genealogy, heraldry, and
others pertinent to genealogy.

Divorce Help Sourcebook. Detroit, Mich.: Gale Research, 1994.

Helps find information needed in all aspects of the divorce process: legal issues, financial matters, professional services, parenting, health
and safety, and so forth. A state-by-state section covers divorce laws,
grounds for divorce, annulment, where to find vital records, and more.

Encyclopedia of Associations. 3 vols. Detroit, Mich.: Gale Research, biennial.

Contains more than 23,000 national and international associations.
Search under such headings as "Veterans," "Hereditary," and "Patriotic
Organizations." Excellent index: numbers refer to entry, not page.
Gives information on when founded, publications, purpose of the asso-
ciation, contact person at time of publication, conferences, conventions,
and meetings. Also has a volume covering international organizations.

Educational Resources Information Center (ERIC). Washington, D.C.: ERIC
Clearinghouse, U.S. Department of Education, Office of Educational
Research and Improvement, 1981.

This is a fiche collection of educational materials indexed in *Resources
in Education* and supported by the U.S. Department of Education.
About 12,000 reports are added every year, with some 300,000 available
now. It is also available online at http://www.aspensys.com/eric/
index.html and very easy to use. Enter *genealogy* and wait for the
results. It breaks into categories, so scroll the screens to find entries for
genealogy. The entries are accessed by ERIC Document (ED) number
and include journal articles as well as reports. There are many reports
on genealogy.

Family Diseases: Are You at Risk? Myra Vanderpool Gormley. Baltimore, Md.:
Genealogical Publishing Co., 1989.

Even though this is published by a genealogical publishing company,
this is an excellent book for any library collection. It gives lots of information necessary for finding out about genetic diseases and how they
can be traced in families.

Gale Directory of Publications and Broadcast Media. 3 vols. Detroit, Mich.:
Gale Research, annual.

This gives geographical access to information on newspapers, magazines, and other publications, alphabetical by state, then city or town, including dates when publications started. Good for locating publications in area of interest if searching for obituaries or marriage and birth notices (small-town newspapers are especially good for gathering this type of material).

Going to America. Terry Coleman. New York: Pantheon Books, 1972.

The story of millions of British and Irish immigrants who came to North America during the middle of the nineteenth century. Tells the story of some of their problems, adventures, and heartbreaks in making the voyage.

Guide to Reference Books. 11th ed. Edited by Robert Balay. Chicago: American Library Association, 1996.

Use the subject listings to find books on genealogy.

Guinness Book of Names. 7th ed. Leslie Alan Dunkling. Enfield, United Kingdom: Guinness Publishing, 1991.

Covers meanings of names, both personal and surnames. It is quite comprehensive in coverage and includes names of ships, streets, trade names, and so forth. No doubt your library already has several books of this type. Make sure to note their locations here.

Immigration History Research Center: A Guide to Collections. University of Minnesota. New York: Greenwood, 1991.

For those people seeking their immigrant ancestors, this gives an insight into the center's holdings and locations of repositories.

National Geographic Index: 1888–1988. Washington, D.C.: National Geographic Society.

Need a picture of a hometown? This might be a good place to start as the *National Geographic* covers the world. It is especially useful in researching an area and for historical background for all parts of the world.

National Union Catalog of Manuscript Collections; Based on Reports from American Repositories of Manuscripts. Ann Arbor, Mich.: J. W. Edwards, 1962–1995.

Cataloging began in 1959, and the first catalog was printed in 1962. There were more than 60,500 collections held by 1,350 different repositories by 1989. When using the index, check under such headings as family papers, genealogy, homesteads, diaries, and so forth. It also indexes by personal, family, corporate, and geographical names. There are no limitations on time, place, or origin. The Library of Congress stopped publishing the hard copy in 1995 and now catalogs directly into the Research Libraries Information Network (RLIN). ArchivesUSA is a CD-ROM—first published by Chadwyck Healy in 1997—that covers this publication and two other manuscript collections: *Directory of Archives and Manuscript Repositories in the United States* (DAMRUS), last published in 1988; and *National*

Inventory of Documentary Sources in the United States (NIDS). There is also Internet access for an additional charge. This will be updated quarterly on the World Wide Web (WWW) and annually on CD-ROM.

New York Public Library Book of How and Where to Look It Up. Sherwood Harris, editor-in-chief. New York: Prentice Hall, 1991.

This covers subject indexes on reference books, telephone sources, government sources, picture sources, special collections, and electronic databases. It has an excellent index.

New York Times. 1858 to date.

One of the better newspapers in the United States. Has an index of all holdings and is a good place to find what happened in the world at any time. Good to give a global perspective to a family history. Be sure to check the advertisements, and you will see what styles were worn, what household furnishings were used, and so forth. Do you know what happened the day you were born? Good place to find out. Most academic libraries will have this in microform from its inception.

Newspapers in Microform: United States, 1948–1983. 2 vols. Washington, D.C.: Library of Congress, 1984.

Used with the *Gale Directory of Publications and Broadcast Media*, this gives information on which libraries hold newspapers in microform, most of which can be acquired by ILL by any library. One volume lists U.S. newspapers, and a companion volume lists foreign newspapers held by U.S. libraries. The symbols used are for the designation given to each library by the Library of Congress. There are some 34,000 titles in 7,457 localities in the United States. Many of the holdings date from the 1700s.

The Oral History Collection of Columbia University. 13 vols. Edited by Elizabeth B. Mason and Louis M. Starr. 3d ed. New York: Oral History Research Office; New York: R. R. Bowker, 1973. Microfiche.

Many university special collections departments, historical societies, and even some libraries have developed oral history programs for interviewing the older inhabitants in their respective areas to add to their local history. Check in areas of interest to find what is available that might add to fleshing out the bones of names and dates.

People's Chronology: A Year by Year Record of Human Events from Prehistory to the Present. Rev. ed. James Trager. New York: Henry Holt and Co., 1992.

A fascinating book to browse by year, decade, or century. Gives some interpretations to the events listed and covers all aspects of human endeavor. Good place to find out what happened the year you were born.

Poole's Index to Periodical Literature. Gloucester, Mass.: Peter Smith, 1802–1906.

This forerunner of the *Reader's Guide to Periodical Literature* covers the late 1800s and early 1900s. Great for early articles on families and local history.

Published Diaries and Letters of American Women: An Annotated Bibliography. Joyce D. Goodfriend. Boston, Mass.: G. K. Hall, 1987.

> Many universities will have this type of material especially if they offer courses in women's studies. Many diaries were written by women on their journeys westward in the covered wagons, and they make interesting reading of the troubles and hardships the women faced. There are many collections of women's diaries; be sure to check the card catalog for additional titles.

Reader's Guide to Periodical Literature. New York: H. W. Wilson, annual, 1901–.

> Starts where *Poole's Index to Periodical Literature* leaves off and covers this type of literature year by year. Divided by subject, it is a great resource for early articles.

Research Centers Directory. Detroit, Mich.: Gale Research, 1990–.

> Gives listing of research centers, making note of their holdings. Includes address, phone numbers, and other pertinent facts.

Timetables of History: A Horizontal Linkage of People and Events. 3d rev. ed. Bernard Grun. New York: A Touchstone Book, 1991.

> Lists events that happened from 5000 B.C. up to 1990, including history, politics, literature, arts, religion, music, science, and more. Excellent for placing ancestors in a time frame.

Township Atlas of the United States, Named Townships. McLean, Va.: Andriot Association, 1977.

> Indexes 22,000 townships that exist today and refers them to detailed maps included in the book. Townships are arranged alphabetically by state, then by counties within the state, and then by the townships within the county. Lists more of the more-modern townships, but does not cover the very early ones. Still, it is very useful.

Travel Guides. Variety of publishers.

> Of the several publishers of this type of material, probably the best known are the Fodor guides. They all cover much the same type of data, so pick the ones best suited to your library. These not only give information on hotels, restaurants, and sightseeing, but also on libraries and repositories in the various countries as well as the gist of their holdings. For patrons going abroad to do genealogy, such guides are a great way to plan a research trip.

Webster's New Geographical Dictionary. Springfield, Mass.: Merriam-Webster, 1988.

> Standardized forms of places and exact locations. Covers current and historical place names and gives location, area, and other information.

Webster's New Biographical Dictionary. Springfield, Mass.: Merriam-Webster, 1983.

Brief sketches of prominent persons in many fields, living and historical.

What Jane Austen Ate and Charles Dickens Knew: From Fox Hunting to Whist—the Facts of Daily Life in Nineteenth-Century England. Daniel Pool. New York: Touchstone, 1993.

This work might be in your collection already. It is a fascinating work detailing life in England during this period and is a must for anyone reading Dickens's novels or those of Jane Austen, the Brontës, or Trollope. It also helps explain some of the terminology of nineteenth-century documents and situations encountered in genealogical research such as currency, the church calendar, apprentices and occupations, what an average house contained, disease, servants, and so forth.

What's in a Name? Leonard R. N. Ashley. Baltimore, Md.: Genealogical Publishing Co., 1989.

This is a more-detailed description of names and covers the historical and multicultural derivation of names. There are many more books out on names, and you may already have some in your library. If so, add them to this list.

Who's Who in America. Chicago: Marquis Who's Who, 1899–.

There are many editions of this, not just *in America*. These cover several disciplines, for example, science, art, nursing, politics, Afro-Americans, military, who was who, and so forth. Also covers areas, such as *Who's Who in the Southwest, Northeast,* and so on. Great sources for short biographical sketches.

World Almanac and Book of Facts. New York: Press Publication Co., annual.

This has a wealth of information and can be used effectively when searching for perpetual calendars; geographical information; chambers of commerce (under state listing, gives a toll-free number for travel information, WWW site address, and other pertinent information state-by-state); a synopsis of world history; zip codes for towns with populations of more than 5,000; statistics; organizations; and so forth. Check the index for other pertinent headings.

Writer's Market. Cincinnati, Ohio: Writer's Digest Books, annual.

Helpful in finding a publisher for a finished work.

Writings on American History. Washington, D.C.: American Historical Association; Millwood, N.Y.: Kraus-Thomson, 1902–1961. (1904–5 and 1941–47 not published.)

This work started out as part of the annual report of the American Historical Association, then became a report on its own. It is arranged by subject and is an excellent way to locate older holdings. There are sections on genealogy and local history, and they are quite complete for the various years represented. Be sure to check other subject areas such as state, military, and so forth. This was followed by the following title.

Writings on American History, 1962–73, a Subject Bibliography of Articles.
Vols. 1–4. Washington, D.C.: American Historical Association, 1962–73.

Continues above title in same format.

Writings on American History: A Subject Bibliography of . . . Washington,
D.C.: American Historical Association, 1973/74–1989/90. Ceased
publication.

This picks up where the preceding title stops and covers the same type
of material in the same format.

SECTION 7

Basic Genealogy Bibliography

The following list of books will prove invaluable in giving service to genealogists. These books will form the basic research collection where many of the answers to the questions genealogists will ask can be found, especially those genealogists just starting their research. You will notice that most of the items on this list center on the location of sources in and around the country and not on the genealogical works themselves.

Another avenue you might take to supplement your collection in genealogy is to apply to state sources for a grant, making sure you note genealogy patron use of your library resources and the need to supplement your holdings to be able to offer adequate service to patrons.

American Genealogical Research at the DAR, Washington, D.C. Eric G. Grundset and Steven B. Rhodes. Washington, D.C.: National Society Daughters of the American Revolution, 1997.

> According to the authors in the introduction, "This new DAR publication serves as a manual discussing the collections at DAR Headquarters in Washington, D.C. within the broader scope of American genealogical sources and subjects. Explaining what is available at DAR and how a researcher will be able to use it in his or her search for their family's place in American history is the book's purpose." The headquarters holds some unique material compiled by the various DAR chapters around the country and deposited here. The material does not circulate, has open stacks, and the staff will do all photocopying.

American Passenger Arrival Records: A Guide to the Records of Immigrants Arriving at American Ports by Sail and Steam. Rev. ed. Michael H. Tepper. Baltimore, Md.: Genealogical Publishing Co., 1993.

> Gives a concise overview of ship lists and notes other types of records that provide immigrant arrival information.

Ancestry's Red Book: American State, County and Town Sources. Edited by Alice Eichholz. Salt Lake City, Utah: Ancestry, 1992.

> For each state, gives a brief history; lists records by type (i.e., vital, land, census, local history, military, maps); and notes libraries, archives,

and societies with addresses. Counties are listed in charts giving date formed and dates vital and court or land records were begun.

Basic Facts about—Heraldry for Family Historians. Iain Swinnerton. Birmingham, England: Federation of Family History Societies, 1995.

Write to the federation at 2–4 Killer Street, Ramsbottom, Bury, Lancs BLO 9BZ, England.

Burke's Genealogical and Heraldic History of the Landed Gentry, Including American Families with British Ancestry. 18th ed. 3 vols. John Bernard Burke. London: Burke's Peerage, 1965–1972.

Burke's Royal Families of the World. 2 vols. London: Burke's Peerage, 1977–.

This author has published many volumes on heraldry and its usage, and these are only two of the many. They cover all aspects of heraldry and the families who are entitled to bear coats of arms.

Celebrating the Family: Steps to Planning a Family Reunion. Vandella Brown. Salt Lake City, Utah: Ancestry, 1991.

Hundreds of family reunions are held each year around the United States and in Canada as well. This book is a basic manual on planning a successful reunion that will unite, entertain, and inspire the celebration.

Cemeteries of the U.S.: A Guide to Contact Information for U.S. Cemeteries and Their Records. Edited by Deborah M. Burek. Detroit, Mich.: Gale Research, 1994.

Contains basic contact information for about 22,000 cemeteries, both in operation and closed. Arrangement is geographic by state, then county. There is also an alphabetical index by cemetery name and place name. Each cemetery entry includes information on founding, name, contact person, address, special services, location of records, historical notes, closing date if applicable, accessibility of records, and some historical features.

The Center: A Guide to Genealogical Research in the National Capital Area. Christina K. Schaefer. Baltimore, Md.: Genealogical Publishing Co., 1996.

The topics covered include federal land records, Library of Congress, National Archives, military records, federal government agencies, District of Columbia, academic institutions, professional societies and organizations with genealogical resources, and areas in Virginia and Maryland. Also includes forms for ordering copies of census records, veterans records, military records, and passenger arrival records, with instructions on how to submit these forms.

Cite Your Sources: A Manual for Documenting Family Histories and Genealogical Records. Richard S. Lackey. Jackson: University Press of Mississippi, 1986.

Even though it is dated, it is an excellent book on how to document a family history and why it is necessary.

A Complement to Genealogies in the Library of Congress: A Bibliography. Compiled and edited by Marion J. Kaminkow. Baltimore, Md.: Magna Carta Book Co., 1981.

> This is a complement to the two volumes published by the Library of Congress—*Genealogies Cataloged by the Library of Congress Since 1986* and *Genealogies in the Library of Congress*—and the three volumes together give a pretty comprehensive listing of family histories.

Dictionary of Heraldry. Edited by Stephen Friar. New York: Harmony Books, 1987.

> Good overall history of heraldry.

Evidence: Citation and Analysis for the Family Historian. Elizabeth Shown Mills. Baltimore, Md.: Genealogical Publishing Co., 1997.

> With today's use of the computer, it is more important to cite your sources in the correct manner. As not every written genealogical material is proved, neither are any data provided by someone on the Internet proven evidence. Someone must be able to check your source, and without the correct uniform resource locator (URL) address, it would be impossible. Very good examples are given for just this type of citation. This book is good not only for genealogy, but for any other citation question for e-mail and Web sites.

Family Reunion Handbook: A Guide to Family Reunion Planning. Barbara Brown and Tom Ninkovich. San Francisco: Reunion Research, 1996.

> Not only covers the budgeting of such an undertaking, but also includes information on starting a family newsletter, record keeping, food, fund-raising, activities for children, and more.

Genealogical and Local History Books in Print. Compiled and edited by Marian Hoffman. Baltimore, Md.: Genealogical Publishing Company, latest edition. Periodically updated.

> This multivolume set contains a family history volume; U.S. sources and resources volumes—an Alabama–New York volume and a North Carolina–Wyoming volume; and a general reference and world resources volume. They are arranged by authors' names or the names of sponsoring institutions. All entries give full title of the work, date of publication, information on whether indexed or illustrated, or cloth or paper, number of pages, selling price, and vendor number. Vendors are listed separately in the front of the book, both numerically and alphabetically, with addresses and special ordering information.

Genealogies Cataloged by the Library of Congress since 1986: With a List of Established Forms of Family Names and a List of Genealogies Converted to Microform since 1983. Washington, D.C.: Cataloging Distribution Service, Library of Congress, 1992.

> With *A Complement to Genealogies in the Library of Congress: A Bibliography* and the following title, this makes a comprehensive listing up to the date of publication. Check the Library of Congress online catalog

(http://www.loc.gov) for holdings after this publication date. This was
issued as a government document and could be housed in that
location.

Genealogies in the Library of Congress. 2 vols. Baltimore, Md.: Genealogical
Publishing Co., 1975.

The Library of Congress is the national repository for all monograph
publications that are under copyright, and all genealogies published
under copyright in the United States go there. Their collection is very
extensive.

Genealogist's Address Book. 3d ed. Elizabeth Petty Bentley. Baltimore, Md.:
Genealogical Publishing Co., 1995.

Includes national, state, ethnic, and religious organizations; adoption
registries; and research centers. Lists historical societies, libraries, and
genealogical societies with hours of operation, phone numbers, addresses, publications if any, plus tidbits of their holdings and other information. If your library has many genealogy patrons, this is a must
for the reference section.

Genealogist's Handbook: Modern Methods for Researching Family History.
Raymond S. Wright. Chicago: American Library Association, 1995.

An excellent book for introducing genealogy to anyone interested in
further pursuit of this hobby. Especially good as a textbook in the
teaching of genealogy.

Genealogy Online: Researching Your Roots. 2d ed. Elizabeth Powell Crowe.
McGraw Hill, 1996.

Technology has changed the way people today do genealogy research.
This book will help you find information on the World Wide Web
(WWW); then, it is up to you what will be of use to you. It does not
teach how to do genealogy, but it does help you do it better through
technology. Discusses electronic mail, bulletin boards, networks, and
echos. One of the better books on the market today.

Genealogy Sourcebook Series. Detroit, Mich.: Gale Research, 1995.

There are four titles in this group: *African American Genealogical
Sourcebook*; *Asian American Genealogical Sourcebook*; *Hispanic American
Genealogical Sourcebook*; and *Native American Genealogical Sourcebook*.
Covers the special research sources for each respective ethnic group.
Includes emigration and migration history; possible problems in interpreting data; basic records such as family, census, and church
records; and a directory of genealogical information, archives and
libraries, organizations, print sources, and other information relative
to ethnic groups.

Generations and Change: Genealogical Perspectives in Social History. Edited
by Robert M. Taylor and Ralph J. Crandall. Macon, Ga.: Mercer University
Press, 1986.

An excellent book to help understand the social aspects and historical perspectives of writing a family history. Demonstrates the close relationship between genealogy, history, and the social sciences and how they all can be used to create an interesting story of family history.

Genograms in Family Assessment. Monica McGoldrick and Randy Gerson. New York: W. W. Norton and Co., 1985.

"A genogram is a format for drawing a family tree that records information about family members and their relationships over at least three generations" (page 1). A genogram gives a graphic way to depict a medical history of at least three generations and how this affects the succeeding ones.

Going to Salt Lake City to Do Family History Research. 3d rev. ed. J. Carlyle Parker. Turlock, Calif.: Marietta Publishing Co., 1996.

This book is essential if one is going to the Mormon Family History Center in Salt Lake City. The amount of material is awe inspiring, and some preparation is needed if one hopes to make the most out of a trip. There is no charge to use this library, though there is a small fee for copying. This book is also helpful in using the Mormon Family History Centers around the United States and elsewhere. The Salt Lake City library has more than 1 million reels of microfilm, 300,000 fiche, and 250,000 volumes of books, adding more each year. Given these numbers, one can see why good preparation is necessary before going.

Guide to Genealogical Research in the National Archives. Washington, D.C.: National Archives and Records Administration, 1985.

The archives published a three-volume set in 1997 to replace this book. Either one of these editions is a must to understand the way the National Archives classifies its holdings. The newer edition gives the holdings that have been transferred to Archives II in College Park, Maryland, and those that have come back to the main archives building. The National Archives is the repository of all federal records, and as such it is a must to locate military pension records, bounty land records, and census records. Really a must for any library that works with genealogy patrons.

Handwriting of American Records for a Period of 300 Years. E. Kay Kirkham. Logan, Utah: Everton Publishers, 1973.

Books of this type are essential for trying to decipher colonial and early American handwriting. Many early American ancestors came from England, and the carryover into the United States is very apparent whether in laws, handwriting, and so forth. The use of abbreviations can be very confusing as well. Remember, the typewriter was not invented until the nineteenth century, so all documents were written by hand. Spelling was not customized as we know it today until much later, and much of the spelling was phonetic.

Heraldry: The Story of Armorial Bearings. Walter Buehr. New York: Putnam, 1964.

This is a good introduction to heraldry and how it is used in arms and armor.

How to Read the Handwriting and Records of Early America. Rev. ed. E. Kay Kirkham. Salt Lake City, Utah: Deseret Book Co., 1965.

This is another publication that can be of enormous help in trying to decipher colonial handwriting.

In Search of . . . [Your Canadian Roots, British and Irish Roots, Scottish Roots, Welsh Roots, and so on].** Angus Baxter. Baltimore, Md.: Genealogical Publishing Co., various editions.

These are just a few of the titles in this series. The books describe how to get started in the various countries, how to use the records and where they are located, census records, church registers, and civil registration. They also include information on the pertinent records in the Mormon Family History Centers.

International Vital Records Handbook. Thomas Jay Kemp. Baltimore, Md.: Genealogical Publishing Co., latest edition.

Lists U.S. records by state with copies of the various forms needed to request birth, marriage, and death certificates. Includes what years are available in each repository and charges for photocopies. These forms vary state-by-state and were in use at the time of the writing of the handbook. Also included are records from the U.S. Trust Territories, Canada, English-speaking Caribbean, British Isles, and related countries and Europe.

Knights and the Age of Chivalry. Raymond Rudorff. New York: Viking, 1974.

The dust jacket claims "this book gives a clear, lively and thoroughly documented account of the origins and development of this astonishing brotherhood of arms." (The children's collection often has colorful books on this topic.)

Land and Property Research in the United States. E. Wade Hone. Salt Lake City, Utah: Ancestry, Inc., 1997.

One of the earliest forms of records, land ownership has been recorded for centuries. Land and property records are probably the most numerous of records. This book covers all factors concerning ownership of land and how to locate such records.

The Library of Congress: A Guide to Genealogical and Historical Research. James C. Neagles and Mark C. Neagles. Salt Lake City: Utah Ancestry, 1990.

An excellent introduction to the holdings of the Library of Congress. Gives a general history of the collection and tips on how to use it, and lists key source materials for regional and state history.

Map Guide to the U.S. Federal Censuses, 1790–1920. William Thorndale and William Dollarhide. Baltimore, Md.: Genealogical Publishing Co., 1988.

Over the course of the history of the United States, state and county boundaries have changed several times. The maps in this book note the changes every ten years to correspond with the federal census taking. Background information summarizes these changes.

Meyer's Directory of Genealogical Societies in the U.S.A. and Canada. Edited by Mary Keysor Meyer. Mt. Airy, Md.: Meyer, various editions.

Alphabetized by state or province, this includes many of the societies, giving basic information, membership information, phone numbers, publications, and so forth.

National Directory of Morticians, the Red Book. Chagrin Falls, Ohio: National Directory of Morticians, annual.

Arranged by state, then city. Canadian listings by province. Includes listing of daily newspapers, airports, airlines, where to obtain death certificates, what information is included in the certificates, foreign consulates in the United States (with phone numbers), what documentation is necessary for shipping remains to foreign countries, National Cemeteries, Veterans Administration Offices with burial benefits, hospitals, and regional offices.

Nearby History: Exploring the Past Around You. David E. Hyvig and Myron A. Marty. Nashville, Tenn.: American Association for State and Local History, 1982.

This book intertwines the family, community, and material cultures and should help readers understand the importance of recording these aspects in a family history. Covers such topics as buildings, neighborhoods, institutions, questions to use to uncover this information, and how to incorporate the results in a more meaningful family history.

The New A to Zax: A Comprehensive Genealogical Dictionary for Genealogists and Historians. 2d ed. Barbara Jean Evans. Champaign, Ill.: author, 1990.

There are several of this type of book on the market today as well as over the WWW. Gives definitions for many of the specialized words used by genealogists as well as the more archaic words and definitions, occupations, Latin terms, and so on. This or one of this type should be a must in any library that tries to aid the genealogist.

Oxford Companion to Local and Family History. Edited by David Hey. Oxford: Oxford University Press, 1996.

Arranged alphabetically, detailed entries are provided on such topics as ecclesiastical, social, urban, agricultural, legal, and family history in the British Isles. It also includes a listing of regnal years, national record offices and counties, and local record offices, with addresses.

Oxford Guide to Heraldry. Thomas Woodcock and John M. Robinson. Toronto: Oxford University Press, 1988.

Another good overall picture of the history of heraldry and its uses.

Researcher's Guide to American Genealogy. Val D. Greenwood. Baltimore, Md.: Genealogical Publishing Co., 1991.

> The best basic guide in genealogical research, more for the advanced researcher than for the beginner. Excellent examples are given to help understand the ins and outs of genealogy.

The Source: A Guidebook of American Genealogy. Edited by Loretta Szucs and Sandra Luebking. Salt Lake City, Utah: Ancestry, 1997.

> This is also a necessary tool for any library. It identifies, locates, and interprets all manner of records used in genealogy research: vital records, cemetery research, marriage records, census records, military records, city directories, ethnic records, computer use, hereditary and lineage societies, and so forth.

They Came in Ships: A Guide to Finding Your Immigrant Ancestor's Arrival Record. Rev. ed. John P. Colletta. Salt Lake City, Utah: Ancestry, Inc., 1993.

> Gives clues on how to locate an immigrant's arrival when no other method works.

Unpuzzling Your Past: A Basic Guide to Genealogy. 3d ed. Emily Anne Croom. Cincinnati, Ohio: Betterway Books, 1995.

> Also published by this author is the *Unpuzzling Your Past Workbook*—essential forms and letters for all genealogists—and *The Genealogist's Companion and Sourcebook*—a beyond-the-basics, hands-on guide to unpuzzling your past. As the first title suggests, it is a basic how-to book. The workbook contains forms and letters that can be copied and adapted for all occasions. The third title is used for the more advanced researcher. One nice thing about these three books is they are generally available in most popular book stores in most areas.

Helpful Classification Schedules: Library of Congress and Dewey

Two main classification systems are used by libraries. Most university libraries use the Library of Congress system, and public libraries in general use the Dewey decimal system. Both use further clarification, known as the Cutter Number, by adding a letter for the initial main entry name with additional numbers for further identification of the author name. The cataloging department should have the tools for the classification system your library uses. Try to borrow a copy and study what other numbers would be helpful to genealogists. Subject heading manuals will also help define the subjects for searching your card catalog, whether online or in card format.

LIBRARY OF CONGRESS

BR 140–1500	Church History
CS 9–25	"How to Books"
CS 25–35	Royal Genealogy
CS 36–40	English Genealogy
CS 41–70	American Genealogy
CS 71–80	Genealogies of American Families
CS 81–99	Canadian Genealogy
CS 100–399	Latin American Genealogy
CS 439	Genealogies of English Families
CS 455–459	Welsh Genealogy
CS 470–479	Scottish Genealogy
CS 480–499	Irish Genealogy
CS 500–570	European Genealogy
CS 580–599	French Genealogy
CS 600–699	German Genealogy
CS 2300–3090	History of Names

CS 3000–3999	Heraldry
D-DD	History, General and Old World
E-F	History of America
F 1–975	United States Local History, e.g.,
F 116–130	New York
F 221–235	Virginia
F 306–320	Florida
G-GB	Geography
GR	Folklore

DEWEY DECIMAL SYSTEM

016	Bibliography
030	General Encyclopedias
360	Patriotic Societies (e.g., Mayflower, Sons of the Revolution, DAR, etc.)
390	Customs and folk life
920	Biography
929.1	Genealogy how to
929.2	Family histories
929.3	Multiple family histories
940	European history
973	United States history
	This is broken down by historical period (e.g., colonial, Revolutionary period, Civil War, etc.).
974-979	Starting here are regional (e.g., northeastern states, southern states, etc.) and state histories. State histories are further broken down by county.

You might want to make a listing of the county breakdowns of your state for easier location of holdings. Add here.

State, County, City, Town, and Area Sources

STATE SOURCES

The state library and archives, the state historical society, and state genealogical society are very valuable resources, and each covers the entire state. Write for information brochures on their services and holdings, listing current hours, contact person, if they accept mail orders and cost, photocopy costs, and so forth. Most state genealogy societies have a conference each year or every other year. Get on their mailing lists to know when one is in your area and try to attend. Many of the conferences offer some lectures on the library and genealogy, and you can pick up some good contacts there as well as good tips to aid your service to patrons. Some state genealogical societies have started to offer a monetary prize for librarians who offer help to genealogists to enable that person to attend one of the national conferences. Check out your state society for its program. Use appendix 16 to add these sources.

COUNTY, CITY, TOWN, AND AREA SOURCES

Know the public libraries in your area and what holdings they have on genealogy and local history. If there is a university in your area that would have the more expensive reference materials and government documents, contact the reference department and find out their policies for usage by the public. Most private universities will not permit walk-ins from the public, and there might be a charge to use the facilities. Public universities, however, do not have such restrictions. Get a listing of their hours as they probably have reduced hours during semester breaks.

Note if there is a genealogy society, Mormon Family History Center, or historical society in the county or town. Check to see if you can be on their mailing lists for their newsletters, seminars, workshops, and program flyers; and note names of contact persons to keep abreast of happenings in your area. Be sure to get good directions to their locations (possibly a map) and information about hours, charges for photocopies, and restrictions to their use by the public. Know the local hereditary societies in your area, the Daughters of the American Revolution (DAR), Sons of the American Revolution (SAR), Colonial Dames, and so on. They can be another source of help in many ways. Encourage them to hold meetings in your library if there is a meeting room available. Keep in touch with their officers and get contact names for their programs. Check your local newspaper for announcements of meetings, workshops, and so forth, and mount them on an announcement board with other meetings in your community. Use appendix 17 to add local listings.

Libraries with Large Genealogical Collections

This is a sampling of public and special libraries with large genealogical collections. Consult the *Directory of Historical Societies and Agencies in the United States and Canada* (Nashville, Tenn.: American Association for State and Local History, latest edition); *Directory of Special Libraries and Information Centers* (Detroit, Mich.: Gale Research, 1998); and the *American Library Directory* (New York: R. R. Bowker, latest edition) for other libraries in other areas of interest. Many of these libraries participate in interlibrary loan (ILL). Check to see if there is a fee for this service. Write for brochures of their services, holdings, charges for photocopies, and if they accept mail requests, and add where appropriate. Most brochures are free of charge.

Allen County Public Library
Fred J. Reynolds Historical Genealogy Department
900 Webster Street
Fort Wayne, IN 46802
(219) 421-1225
http://www.acpl.lib.in.us
Curt Witcher, Manager, Fred J. Reynolds Historical Genealogy Department

> Houses one of the largest genealogy collections in the United States and actively adds to its collection. Holdings cover most of the United States as well as Canada, England, Scotland, Ireland, and Wales. Publishes *Periodical Source Index (PERSI)*—"the largest and most widely used index of genealogical and historical periodical articles in the world," according to their brochure. The library owns all titles mentioned in *PERSI*, and you can write to them or go through ILL to obtain a copy of an article. There is a charge for this service. *PERSI* is a subject index to genealogy and local history periodicals written in English and French-Canadian since 1800. In print, it is 27 volumes. It is also available in CD-ROM for $99.95 (1997) from Ancestry.com, 266 W. Center Street, Orem, UT 84057. The CD-ROM is very user friendly and easy to use.

Brigham Young University
Harold B. Lee Library
Provo, UT 84602
(801) 378-6091

> Has a very large genealogical collection and holds genealogical classes as
> well as conferences. Much of the collection is available through ILL from
> your public library.

Connecticut Historical Society Library
One Elizabeth Street
Hartford, CT 06105
(860) 236-5621
FAX: (860) 236-2664

> Very large collection of material on all of New England, especially strong
> on Connecticut.

Connecticut State Library
History and Genealogy Unit
231 Capitol Avenue
(860) 566-3692
FAX: (860) 566-2133
http://www.cslnet.ctstateu.edu/handg.htm
Hartford, CT 06106

> This is a must for anyone with Connecticut ancestors, whether they settled
> there or just passed through.

Dallas Public Library
Genealogy Section
1515 Young Street
Dallas, TX 75201
(214) 670-1433
http://www.lib.ci.dallas.tx.us

> As one would expect, the library is very bountiful in holdings on Texas,
> covering all aspects of its varied past.

Detroit Public Library
Burton Historical Collection
5201 Woodward Avenue
Detroit, MI 48202
(313) 833-1480
http://www.detroit.lib.mi.us/

> This collection is national in scope with special emphasis on the Michigan
> area. Also houses the Burton Historical Collection, which is very strong
> both in genealogy and history for the old northwest.

Ellen Payne Odom Genealogy Library
204 5th Street SE
Moultrie, GA 31768

Mailing address: P.O. Box 1110
Moultrie, GA 31776-1110
(912) 985-6540
FAX: (912) 985-0936

Home for most of the Scottish clan information in the United States as well as a good Southern collection. They publish a free newspaper called *Family Tree;* write to be added to their subscriber list. There is also an online version of the newspaper at http://www.teleport.com/~binder/famtree.shtml.

Family History Library of the Church of Jesus Christ of Latter-day Saints

Genealogical Society of Utah
35 North West Temple
Salt Lake City, UT 84150
(801) 240-2331

Possibly the largest genealogy library in the world, with Mormon Family History Centers throughout the world. Check your local phone book under Church of Jesus Christ of Latter-day Saints for one in your location. Microfilm copies of the main library's holdings can be accessed through your local Mormon Family History Center, for use in the center only. The centers also have genealogical forms as well as other material available for purchase. One excellent series is the research guide for each of the states and many countries. It lists all the Mormon Family History Centers in each state as well as the archives and libraries of interest, information on Bible records, biographies, cemeteries, census records, church records, court records, emigration records, and many more. These are available for about $1 each and are gold mines of information. Try to find one for your state, and this could answer many of the questions you are asked. Microfilm teams have been around the world making copies of all kinds of records. One very helpful series is the International Genealogical Index (IGI), which lists births, christenings, and marriages. This lists more than 200 million names, so you can see the value of searching this early in your research. Very few if any deaths will be found, though a will or two might appear. The Ancestral File has more than 20 million names on family trees that have been submitted to the library. The centers are heavily used and space might be at a premium, so phone ahead to determine the status of the one in your area.

Friends Historical Library of Swarthmore College

500 College Avenue
Swarthmore, PA 19081
(610) 328-8496

Holds one of the largest collection of Quaker materials in the world. Covers most Quaker meetings in the United States.

The Holland Society of New York Library

122 E. 58th Street
New York, NY 10022
(212) 758-1875

This library specializes in Dutch genealogy for the mid-Atlantic states as well as other areas and is the largest of its kind.

Houston Public Library
Clayton Library, Center for Genealogical Research
5300 Caroline
Houston, TX 77004-6896
(713) 524-0101
http://sparc.hpl.lib.tx.us/hpl/Clayton.html.

> Excellent coverage of all related genealogical materials—censuses, maps, periodicals, and reference material—and still growing.

Johns Hopkins University
George Peabody Library
17 East Mount Vernon Place
Baltimore, MD 21202
(410) 659-8179

> One of the largest collections of British parish records as well as other British material in America.

Library of Congress
Local History and Genealogy Reading Room, Thomas Jefferson Building
10 First Street SE
Washington, DC 20540-5554
(202) 707-5537
http://lcweb.loc.gov

> This institution should need no introduction. All copyrighted material is housed in the Library of Congress, and it is the central place to deposit copies of finished and published genealogical writings.

Mid-Continent Public Library
15616 East Highway 24
Independence, MO 64050
(816) 836-5200
http://www.mcpl.lib.mo.us/

> Has national scope in its collection. Includes a circulating collection that can be accessed by ILL from any public library. Write for a free catalog of their lending collection: Martha L. Meyers, Kermit B. Karns, and Michael C. Henderson, comps., *Genealogy from the Heartland: A Catalog of Titles in the Mid-Continent Public Library Genealogy Circulating Collection* (Independence, Mo.: Mid-Continent Public Library, 1996). The library also published *Interlibrary Loan Sources: A Guide for Librarians and Genealogists*, in January 1997. This also is free and has lots of great hints on how to use ILL to locate materials for your patrons.

National Genealogical Society Library
4527 N. 17th Street
Arlington, VA 22207-2363
(703) 525-0050
http://www.genealogy.org./~ngs

> Has a lending library for members of the society. Publishes a book loan catalog, and their collection is extensive. Also has quite a selection of books for sale.

National Society Daughters of the American Revolution (DAR)
1776 D Street NW
Washington, DC 20006-5392
(202) 879-3229
http://www.dar.org

> Collection is noncirculating. The library is closed to outsiders in April, when the DAR National Convention is held. Houses a unique collection that can not be found at any other site as well as a general genealogical collection that is quite extensive. Each DAR chapter publishes many types of material, including abstracts of wills, cemetery inscriptions, and indexes of reported marked graves of Revolutionary soldiers and their spouses, among other projects. This is the only place much of this material is housed for patron use. The society also has all the lineage papers for membership in the DAR, and copies of these can be obtained. Check as to charge.

New England Historic Genealogical Society
101 Newbury Street
Boston, MA 02116
(617) 536-5740
http://www.nehgs.org

> Very strong in New England but also has material from other areas of the country as well. Has a large collection of English records. There is a lending library for members of the society, with a charge for this service.

New York Public Library
Research Libraries, U.S. History, Local History, and Genealogy Division
5th Avenue and 42nd Street
New York, NY 10018
(212) 930-0828

> One of the largest genealogical collections in the United States.

Newberry Library
60 W. Walton Street
Chicago, IL 60610
(312) 943-9090
http://www.newberry.org

> Large North American local and family history collection.

State Historical Society of Wisconsin
816 State Street
Madison, WI 53706
(608) 264-6535
http://www.wisc.edu/shs-library/gen.html

> Large North American collection.

Sutro Library
480 Winston Drive
San Francisco, CA 94132
(415) 557-0421
http://sfpl.lib.ca.us/gencoll/gencolsu.htm

A branch of the California State Library, this library houses the largest collection of genealogical material west of Salt Lake City. Material covers a wide range of historical and genealogical material from other states and countries. This library also participates in ILL with most of its materials.

Western Reserve Historical Society Library
10825 East Boulevard
Cleveland, OH 44106
(216) 721-5722
http://www.wrhs.org/library.asp

Has a large collection of books and family histories for areas from New England to Georgia and west to the Mississippi River. Has a large census collection for most of the states.

National Genealogical Societies

There are genealogical societies in every state in the Union as well as in many counties and areas. There are also many historical societies that have excellent resources of state, county, or local histories. Check Elizabeth Petty Bentley, *Genealogist's Address Book* (Baltimore, Md.: Genealogical Publishing Co., 1996); and the *Directory of Historical Societies and Agencies in the United States and Canada*, 22d ed., 2 vols. (Detroit, Mich.: Gale Research, 1997), for particulars of each organization. Check for those in your area, and note the addresses, phone numbers, hours of operation, contact person, and so forth.

Federation of Genealogical Societies
P.O. Box 830220
Richardson, TX 75083-0220
(972) 907-9727
FAX: (972) 907-0299
E-mail: fgs-office@fgs.org
http://www.fgs.org

> This society is unique in that its members consist of genealogical societies rather than individual members. It has a yearly conference in the United States that is open to all genealogists. If your society is a member, there is a price break. Publishes a journal, *Forum*, that gives lots of news of the genealogical world, such as a calendar of events, state reporting, information about family associations, and helpful articles on genealogy.

Genealogical Society of Utah: Family History Library of the Church of Jesus Christ of Latter-day Saints
35 North West Temple
Salt Lake City, UT 84150
(801) 240-2331

> Works closely with the Family History Library of the Church of Jesus Christ of Latter-day Saints. The Genealogical Society of Utah is the acquisitions section of the Family History Library. Membership is limited to the employees of the church. It does not provide individual research.

National Genealogical Society

4527 17th Street N
Arlington, VA 22207-2399
http://www.genealogy.org/~ngs/

> Has a genealogical conference yearly in various states that is well attended, with a large number of vendors selling a variety of genealogical items, books, CD-ROMs, programs, and so forth. Publishes the *National Genealogical Society Quarterly* as well as the *NGS Newsletter,* which incorporates the *NGS/CIG Digest* with news of the computer world. Also has a circulating library for members.

New England Historic Genealogical Society

101 Newbury Street
Boston, MA 02116-3007
http://www.nehgs.org

> Publishes *New England Historical and Genealogical Register,* a quarterly and the oldest genealogical magazine published in the United States (begun in 1847). Also publishes *NEHGS Nexus,* which is a bimonthly publication noting what's new at the society, educational programs being offered, new books and a few articles on genealogy research, genealogies in progress, and some queries.

New York Genealogical and Biographical Society

122 E. 58th Street
New York, NY 10022

> Especially strong in holdings on New York, including Long Island. Publishes the *New York Biographical and Genealogical Record.*

SECTION 12

Genealogical Book Publishers

This is not a complete list by any means as many other publishers publish in this field from time to time. These are the major genealogical book publishers.

Ancestry.com
Department FM 95
P.O. Box 476
Salt Lake City, UT 84110-0476
(800) 531-1790

Ancestry.com
266 W. Center Street
Orem, UT 84057
(801) 426-3500
http://www.ancestry.com

 Publishes books; a journal, *Ancestry*, that has excellent tips on how to do genealogy; computer programs; and more.

Clearfield Company
200 E. Eager Street
Baltimore, MD 21202
(410) 625-9004

 Specializes in reprints.

Everton Publishers
P.O. Box 368
Logan, UT 84323-0368
(435) 752-6022
E-mail: bob@everton.com

Family Line Publications
Rear 63 E. Main Street
Westminster, MD 21157
(800) 876-6103
(410) 876-6101

 Genealogy sourcebooks for Delaware, Maryland, New Jersey, North Carolina, Pennsylvania, Virginia, West Virginia, and Washington, D.C.

Gateway Press, Inc.
1001 N. Calvert Street
Baltimore, MD 21202
(410) 837-8271

> Excellent for helping first-time authors in publishing their works. Write for a free brochure, "A Guide for Authors."

Genealogy Publishing Company
101 N. Calvert Street
Baltimore, MD 21202
(800) 296-6687
FAX: (410) 752-8492

> The premier genealogical publisher.

Heritage Books, Inc.
1540 E. Pointer Ridge Place
Bowie, MD 20716
(800) 398-7709
http://www.heritagebooks.com

Newbury Street Press
D. Brenton Simons, Editor
101 Newbury Street, 2d Floor
Boston, MA 02116-3007
(617) 536-5740, ext. 203
FAX: (617) 536-7303

> Division of the New England Historic Genealogical Society. Publishes high-quality privately sponsored genealogies.

Oryx Press
P.O. Box 33889
Phoenix, AZ 85067-3889
(800) 279-6799
FAX: (800) 279-4663
E-mail: Info@oryx.com
http://www.oryxpress.com/catgen.htm

> Noted for its well-researched publications on a variety of topics.

Picton Press
P.O. Box 250
Rockport, ME 04856-0250
(207) 236-6565; (800) 742-8667
FAX: (207) 366-6713

> Specializes in New England, New York, Virginia, and West Virginia.

Scholarly Resources, Inc.
104 Greenhill Avenue
Wilmington, DE 19805-1897
(800) 772-8937
E-mail: scholres@ssnet.com

You might not think of this publisher as a resource for genealogical materials but they do publish some material, such as Ira A. Glazier's *Italians to America: Lists of Passengers Arriving at U.S. Ports, 1880–1899;* David H. Pratt's *Researching British Probates, 1354–1858;* and Donna Bingham Munger's *Pennsylvania Land Records: A History and Guide for Research,* to name a few. Check their catalog for more titles. They have also been at the last couple of genealogy conferences that I have attended.

University Microfilms International
300 Zeeb Road
Ann Arbor, MI 48106-1346
(800) 521-0600

Part of their research collection is *A Comprehensive Treasury of Family Lineages and Local Histories.* There is a three-part catalog listing all these holdings. For the most part, this collection is on fiche. To house this collection, you would need deep pockets to pay for it as well as enormous space to house the thousands of microfiche and the cabinets. It does come in parts, however, and you could purchase the section that pertains to your area. This could be a prime subject for a grant proposal.

SECTION 13

Book Dealers and Suppliers

BOOK DEALERS

Each book dealer and publisher has catalogs of their books for sale. For most, there is no charge to be put on the mailing list. Keep these catalogs handy for reference by patrons, and check to see what might be a welcome addition to your own collection.

American Genealogical Lending Library (AGLL)
P.O. Box 329
Bountiful, UT 84011-0329
(800) 760-AGLL
FAX: (801) 298-5468
http://www.agll.com

> Lends microfilm and fiche for a charge.

Appleton's Books and Genealogy
Tower Place Mall
8700 Pineville-Matthews Road, No. 610
Charlotte, NC 28226
(800) 777-3601
http://www.appletons.com

> As well as new genealogy books, genealogy software, and CD-ROMs, this shop offers a selection of used books and a book search service.

Family Line Publications
Rear 63 E. Main Street
Westminster, MD 21157
(800) 876-6103

> Genealogical sourcebooks for Delaware, Maryland, New Jersey, North Carolina, Pennsylvania, Virginia, West Virginia, and Washington, D.C. Also works with authors on publications projects.

Genealogy House
3148 Kentucky Avenue S
Minneapolis, MN 55426-3471
(612) 920-6990

> Sells books, maps, forms, and pedigree charts.

Hearthstone Bookshop
5735-A Telegraph Road
Alexandria, VA 22303
(703) 960-0087
FAX: (703) 960-0087
E-mail: info@hearthstonebooks.com
http://www.hearthstonebooks.com

> Attends most major genealogy conferences with a great selection of books.
> Sends monthly newsletters covering new books and a list of those books in
> short supply.

Higginson Book Company
148-AB Washington Street
P.O. Box 778
Salem, MA 01970
(508) 745-7170

> Reprints genealogies and local histories; a family history catalog and a
> source catalog give their listings. There is a charge for their catalogs. Check
> their online catalog at http://www.higginsonbooks.com.

Hoenstine Rental Library
414 Montgomery Street
Holidaysburg, PA 16648
(814) 695-0632

> Specializes in Pennsylvania history and genealogy. One of the few libraries
> of genealogical material that loans material.

Tuttle Antiquarian Books, Inc.
28 S. Main Street
P.O. Box 541
Rutland, VT 05701
(802) 773-8229
FAX: (802) 773-1493
E-mail: Tuttbook@Interloc.com

> They publish a lengthy catalog, and the price in 1997 was $7.50. Many of
> the items are secondhand books in good condition and probably not avail-
> able anywhere else. There are also reprints listed, and many of these books
> are older and long out-of-print. Each entry gives the bibliographic informa-
> tion as well as a two- or three-word status of the book—whether photo-
> copy or reprint, worn, in good condition, and so forth.

SUPPLIERS   Many local genealogical societies and Mormon Family History Centers will have a supply of various forms for purchase. Contact them to verify what forms are available and the price and add the information here.

Skeleton Closet
P.O. Box 91392
Louisville, KY 40291-0392
(502) 239-0480

> Sells all kinds of forms and research aids. Write for their catalog. They also have a speakers bureau and will give workshops. Present at most genealogical conferences.

Willow Bend Books
28–18 Ft. Evans Road NE, No. 101
Leesburg, VA 20176-4429
FAX: (703) 443-9203
E-mail: willowbend@mediasoft.net
http://server.mediasoft.net/ScottC

> This Internet bookstore handles many different publishers, all through its web site.

Ye Olde Genealogie Shoppe
P.O. Box 39128
Indianapolis, IN 46239
(800) 419-0200

> As well as forms, this company lists quite a variety of birth, marriage, and death records for sale, plus lots of how-tos. Write for their catalog and be put on their mailing list. Usually attends most major genealogical conferences as well as many local ones.

Add other companies here as you find them.

National Archives, Branches, and Presidential Libraries

NATIONAL ARCHIVES

The National Archives and Records Administration (NARA) is the main repository of records of the U.S. government. Although it is an adventure to go to Washington to view the records in person, you are also able to acquire many of the records by mail. Many of these records require a special form to access. Write to the archives to acquire the appropriate form. If you travel to Washington, go to the archives entrance on Pennsylvania Avenue. You must obtain an identification card for entry into the building. There is no charge for this card, valid for one calendar year, but you will need a valid driver's license showing your photo and address to obtain one.

Much of the information is viewed on microfilm, and the microfilm reading room is on the fourth floor. It is advisable to get there early in the day as the microfilm readers are in great demand. The main reading room is on the second floor, and here you can view original documents. You are not permitted to bring anything into the room other than paper and pencil and a small change purse, but there are plenty of lockers outside where you can store pocketbooks, notebooks, and so forth. The charge is a quarter, which you get back when you return the key to the locker. Your material will be searched on entering and leaving the reading room as well as the building. The entrance on Constitution Avenue is the showroom, where you can see the Constitution of the United States, and there is a gift shop. The web site has a wealth of information to browse as well as the research guides to most of the records housed there. The archives also publishes *The Record: News from the National Archives and Records Administration.* It is published five times a year at no charge and brings to the public activities, stories on holdings, and the latest microfilm releases of interest to genealogists.

National Archives
7th Street and Pennsylvania Avenue NW
Washington, D.C. 20408-0001
(202) 501-5400
E-mail: inquire@nara.gov
http://www.nara.gov/
    The archives has opened a second branch, at College Park, Maryland.

National Archives at College Park (Archives II)
8601 Adelphi Road
College Park, MD 20740-6001
(301) 713-6800

BRANCHES   There are several branches of the National Archives that house many of the same records as the main building (e.g., censuses, etc.) but also center on the records of the various areas they serve. These are known as the National Archives Regional Branches (NARB), and addresses follow, along with the regions they serve.

Washington National Records Center
4205 Suitland Road
Suitland, MD 20746-8001
(301) 457-7000

NARA—Northeast Region (Boston)
380 Trapelo Road
Waltham, MA 02154-6399
(617) 647-8100

    Maine, Vermont, New Hampshire, Massachusetts, Rhode Island, and Connecticut

NARA—Northeast Region (Pittsfield)
100 Dan Fox Drive
Pittsfield, MA 02101-8230
(413) 445-6885

    Maine, Vermont, New Hampshire, Massachusetts, Rhode Island, and Connecticut

NARA—Northeast Region (New York City)
201 Varick Street
New York, NY 10014-4811
(212) 337-1300

    New York, New Jersey, Puerto Rico, and the Virgin Islands

NARA—Mid-Atlantic Region (Center City Philadelphia)
900 Market Street, Room 1350
Philadelphia, PA 19107-4292
(215) 597-3000

    Delaware, Maryland, Pennsylvania, Virginia, and West Virginia

NARA—Southeast Region
1557 St. Joseph Avenue
East Point, GA 30344-2593
(404) 763-7477

Georgia, Alabama, Florida, Kentucky, Mississippi, Tennessee, North Carolina, and South Carolina

NARA—Great Lakes Region (Chicago)
7358 S. Pulaski Road
Chicago, IL 60629-5898
(312) 581-7816

Illinois, Indiana, Michigan, Minnesota, Ohio, and Wisconsin

NARA—Central Plains Region
2312 E. Bannister Road
Kansas City, MO 64131-3060
(816) 926-6934

Iowa, Kansas, Missouri, and Nebraska

NARA—Southwest Region
501 W. Felix Street, Bldg. 1
P.O. Box 6216
Fort Worth, TX 76115-0216
(817) 334-5525

Arkansas, Louisiana, New Mexico, Oklahoma, and Texas

NARA—Rocky Mountain Region
Bldg. 48, Denver Federal Center
P.O. Box 25307
Denver, CO 80225-0307
(303) 236-0801

Colorado, Montana, North Dakota, South Dakota, Utah, and Wyoming

NARA—Pacific Region (Laguna Niguel)
24000 Avila Road
P.O. Box 6719
Laguna Niguel, CA 92607-6719
(714) 360-2641

Arizona, Southern California, and part of Nevada

NARA—Pacific Region (San Francisco)
1000 Commodore Drive
San Bruno, CA 94066-2350
(415) 876-9018

Hawaii, part of Nevada, Northern California, and American Samoa

NARA—Pacific Alaska Region (Anchorage)
654 W. Third Avenue
Anchorage, AK 99501-2145
(907) 271-2443
    Alaska

NARA—Pacific Alaska Region (Seattle)
6125 Sand Point Way NE
Seattle, WA 98115-7999
(206) 526-6507
    Alaska, Idaho, Oregon, and Washington

NARA—National Personnel Records Center
(Civilian Personnel Records)
111 Winnebago Street
St. Louis, MO 63118-4199
FAX: (314) 425-5719
E-mail: center@cpr.nara.gov

NARA—National Personnel Records Center
(Military Personnel Records)
9700 Page Avenue
St. Louis, MO 63132-5100
(314) 538-4201

PRESIDENTIAL LIBRARIES

The presidential library system came into being in 1939, when President Franklin D. Roosevelt donated his personal and presidential papers to the federal government. He also donated part of his estate at Hyde Park to the United States. Funds were raised to construct a library and museum building. He asked the National Archives to take custody of and administer his library.

There are ten presidential libraries, and holdings reflect the personalities of each of the presidents. Holdings include textual materials, photographs, motion pictures, videotapes, and museum objects.

Various associates of each president—including cabinet officials, envoys of foreign governments, political party associates, personal friends, and family members—have donated materials. Check http://www.nara.gov/nara/president/overview.html for additional information. There are links to each of the libraries.

Herbert Hoover Library
210 Parkside Drive
P.O. Box 488
West Branch, IA 52358-0488
(319) 643-5301
FAX: (319) 643-5825
E-mail: library@hoover.nara.gov

Franklin D. Roosevelt Library
511 Albany Post Road
Hyde Park, NY 12538-1999
(914) 229-8114
FAX: (914) 229-0872
E-mail: library@roosevelt.nara.gov

Harry S. Truman Library
100 W. U.S. Highway 24
Independence, MO 64050-1798
(816) 833-1400
FAX: (816) 833-5825
E-mail: library@truman.nara.gov

Dwight D. Eisenhower Library
200 S.E. 4th Street
Abilene, KS 67410-2900
(785) 263-4751
FAX: (785) 263-4751
E-mail: library@eisenhower.nara.gov

John Fitzgerald Kennedy Library
Columbia Point
Boston, MA 02125-3398
(617) 929-4500
FAX: (617) 929-4538
E-mail: library@kennedy.nara.gov

Lyndon Baines Johnson Library
2313 Red River Street
Austin, TX 78705-5702
(512) 916-5137
FAX: (512) 478-9104
E-mail: library@johnson.nara.gov

Nixon Presidential Materials Staff
National Archives at College Park
8601 Adelphi Road
College Park, MD 20740-6001
(301) 713-6950
FAX: (301) 713-6950
E-mail: nixon@arch2.nara.gov

Gerald R. Ford Library
1000 Beal Avenue
Ann Arbor, MI 48109-2114
(734) 741-2218
FAX: (734) 741-2341
E-mail: library@fordlib.nara.gov

Gerald R. Ford Museum
303 Pearl Street NW
Grand Rapids, MI 49504-5353
(616) 451-9263
FAX: (616) 451-9570
E-mail: information.museum@
        fordmus.nara.gov

Jimmy Carter Library
441 Freedom Parkway
Atlanta, GA 30307-1406
(404) 331-3942
FAX: (404) 730-2215
E-mail: library@carter.nara.gov

Ronald Reagan Library
40 Presidential Drive
Simi Valley, CA 93065-0666
(805) 522-8444
FAX: (805) 522-9621
E-mail: library@reagan.nara.gov

George Bush Library
1000 George Bush Drive W
College Station, TX 77843
(409) 260-9554
FAX: (409) 260-9557
E-mail: library@bush.nara.gov

SECTION 15

Education, Conferences, Workshops, and Seminars

Most of the national societies have a yearly conference or workshops throughout the year or both. You can keep abreast of them through your local genealogical society as well as through such genealogical journals as *Everton's Genealogical Helper, Heritage Quest,* or any of the various societies' journals and newsletters.

Association of Professional Genealogists
P.O. Box 11601
Salt Lake City, UT 84147-1601
(504) 766-3018

> Provides a listing of professional genealogists for speakers and for personal research.

Board of Certification of Genealogists
P.O. Box 14291
Washington, DC 20044
http://www.genealogy.org/~bcg/

> Administers certification examinations to qualify as a "certified genealogist" (C.G.) or a "certified genealogical record searcher" (C.G.R.S.). The board also maintains a listing of professional genealogists.

Carl Sandburg College
Attn.: Michael Neill
2232 S. Lake Storey Road
Galesburg, IL 61401
(309) 341-5260
http://www.asc.csc.cc.il.us/~mneill/csc/index.html

> Offers beginning and intermediate online classes in genealogy. Questions should be directed to the instructor, Michael Neill, at michaeln@ misslink.net.

Elderhostel
75 Federal Street
Boston, MA 02110-1941
(617) 426-7788
FAX: (617) 426-8351
http://www.elderhostel.org

Elderhostel offers programs in England, Germany, Ireland, and the United States and is a great way to extend your research. You must be age 60 or older, costs are modest, and it is a great way to meet others doing the same research as you are. Write to the above address to be put on the mailing list for the Elderhostel catalog. You stay at various educational institutions, facilities are adequate, and the charge usually includes room, board, and tuition.

Federation of Genealogical Societies
P.O. Box 830220
Richardson, TX 75083-0220
(972) 907-9727
FAX: (972) 907-9727
E-mail: fgs-office@fgs.org
http://www.fgs.org/~fgs

This organization is composed of genealogy societies across the United States, and it also has a yearly conference. The emphasis here is on the society: how to run a successful society, gain new members, and write effective newsletters, as well as several days of how-to lectures. Many vendors are present here as well.

GENTECH
P.O. Box 28021
Dallas, TX 75228
http://gentech.org

GENTECH has an annual conference on genealogy and technology, and most of the topics deal in some way with computer applications to genealogy. It also hosts sessions at the major genealogical conferences.

National Genealogical Society
Glebe House
4527 17th Street N
Arlington, VA 22207-2399
(703) 525-0050
(800) 473-0060
FAX: (703) 525-0052
E-mail: ngs@ngsgenealogy.org
http://www.ngsgenealogy.org

Holds a yearly conference in various sections of the United States with hourly lectures on various aspects of genealogy. The conference usually lasts about five days, and lots of vendors sell books, CD-ROMs, maps, forms, and more. Great camaraderie among the participants. The society also has a home-study course that is very good and a great introduction to the study of genealogy—"American Genealogy: A Basic Course." There are sixteen lessons in the course, you work with an instructor, and upon completion you receive a certificate. As a student, you set your own pace for completion. There is a lending library for members.

National Institute on Genealogical Research
P.O. Box 14274
Washington, DC 20044-4274

The National Archives is the site of this weeklong seminar, usually held in July of each year. Limited to forty participants, it is not for beginners. Offers daily lectures on various archives records and how to use them effectively, and includes trips to the National Society Daughters of the American Revolution (DAR) Library, Library of Congress, and to the Archives II site. Time is set aside for personal research.

Samford University
Institute of Genealogy and Historical Research
800 Lakeshore Drive
Birmingham, AL 35229
(205) 870-2749

Check with the university for dates and courses offered. It is the American Genealogical Society depository and headquarters.

Many local, state, and regional societies offer beginning workshops and seminars as well as more advanced offerings during the year. The Internet also has beginning courses that you can register for and participate in via your computer. Many of these online courses are free; you just have to register before access is permitted. Contact your local society for programs of its offerings.

Enter information here for your local societies.

Computer Programs and Databases and the Internet

COMPUTER PROGRAMS AND DATABASES

There are a multitude of genealogy programs available for the computer. People can become very passionate about a program they use and find suits their needs; however, a lot depends on the level of expertise users have in working with a computer and how much they want the program to do for them. Today, there are programs that permit audio, scan photographs and other media into a program, provide easy data entry, can develop customized reports, allow Genealogical Data Communication (GEDCOM) import and export, and *more*. It seems each new program promises and delivers more and more. Where will it all end?

Anyway, users must determine for themselves what they want and need in a program. Computer Interest Groups (CIGs) have sprung up all over the country and are very active in helping members understand specific programs. Software programs are an excellent way to keep your genealogy research on track and help sort out all the relationships. Most of the programs now require Windows 95 and lots of memory, depending on the size of the database. Many programs can be purchased in such local computer or office supply stores as Babbage, CompUSA, Office Depot, and others.

Many libraries also have INFOTRAC, an online source for journal articles, some in full text. This database allows flexibility in searching, and the patron can manipulate the search by entering words or phrases relating to genealogical research. Magazine Collection has been integrated with INFOTRAC and can provide full-text capability for about 400,000 articles, where patrons can download the articles they want and have immediate hard copies. INFOTRAC comes with an academic as well as a public library edition, and the academic version has the more scholarly journal titles. Some other databases of this sort are ABI INFORM, BUSINESS INDEX, WILSON combined indexes, and ERIC. Be familiar with the subject headings for genealogical research, and know the ins and outs on how to use them. These types of program are quite a step above searching the *Reader's Guide* or other hard-copy indexes year-by-year, locating the journal article in question, and photocopying it or going through interlibrary loan (ILL) and waiting for delivery.

Genealogical Programs

Following is a partial list of some of the genealogical programs available. Many are available wherever computer programs are sold.

Brothers Keeper for Windows
John Steed
6907 Childsdale Avenue
Rockford, MI 49341
(616) 364-1127

Family Origins Version 5.0
Parsons Technology
One Parsons Drive
P.O. Box 100
Hiawatha, IA 52233-0100
(800) 223-6925

Family Tree Maker
Broderbund Software
P.O. Box 6125
Novato, CA 94947-6125.
(415) 382-4770

The Master Genealogist Version 1.2
Wholly Genes
6868 Ducketts Lane
Elk Ridge, MD 21227
(800) 982-2103

Personal Ancestral File (PAF),
  MS-DOS Version 2.31;
  Mac Version 2.3.1
LDS Church Distribution Center
1999 W. 1700 S
Salt Lake City, UT 84150
(800) 537-5950

> Produced by the Family History Center of the Church of Jesus Christ of Latter-day Saints.

Reunion Version 4
Leister Productions
P.O. 289
Mechanicsburg, PA 17055
(717) 697-1378

Ultimate Family Tree
Palladium Interactive
743 E. Franklin Street, Suite B
Spencer, IN 47460
(812) 829-4405

> Palladium Interactive took over the company that produced Roots programs, which had been a staple for years. The deluxe edition is able to do almost anything and everything wanted in a software program.

THE INTERNET

If you have a Freenet available in your area, add that address here, and know how to access it to get to the Internet.

The following is only a sampling of e-mail and World Wide Web (WWW) sources. New sites are launched almost every week and can usually be found through the linking choice of other web sites. Sites from all over the world can be accessed through these same sites as well. Bookmark your favorite ones, but remember that addresses for these sites can change. If you find a change in any of the addresses, be sure to note it and update your bookmark. Be careful in downloading any files as all material on the Internet falls under copyright, but the uniform resource locator (URL) address itself does not.

A couple of books have recently been published concerning the WWW and genealogy. One is Thomas Jay Kemp's *Virtual Roots: A Guide to Genealogy and Local History on the World Wide Web* (Wilmington, Del.: Scholarly Resources, 1997). It comes in both hardback ($65) and paperback ($24.95). There is a short introduction, and the rest of the book is made up of web sites. Another book is Cyndi Howells's *Netting Your Ancestors: Genealogical Research on the Internet* (Baltimore, Md.: Genealogical Publishing Co., 1997) at $19.95. This is by the owner of one of the most successful web sites, Cyndi's List of Genealogy Sites (her WWW address follows). This is a much more useful book in that it explains how to use the Internet, e-mail, mailing lists, and news groups; how to download; and more. She gives tips on what hardware and software you need—tools for getting online. This seems a better buy and is not likely to go out of date as quickly as the other book might.

E-mail Addresses

Genbrit-L

To subscribe, send an e-mail to Genbrit-L@apple.rootsweb.com, with *subscribe* as the only word in the body of the message. If you seek English, Welsh, or Scottish ancestors, this would be the list for you. As with Roots-L, you can choose either each message or digest format. Note that the amount of traffic on both of these lists can be daunting, and the digest mode is preferable.

GENMTD-L

Subscribe to LISTSERV@LISTSERV.NET. The message text should be *subscribe GENMTD-L*. This list is geared to methods of research rather than to questions on family searches.

Librarians Serving Genealogists

Subscribe to listserv@nosferatu.cas.usf.edu. Leave the subject line blank, and in the body of the message put only *subscribe genealib* and your first and last name. Send messages to genealib@nosferatu.cas.usf.edu. There is also a web site for this list—http://www.cas.usf.edu/lis/genealib—with links to lots of other information that is of use to librarians. This rather recent list will aid with questions from librarians who are involved in helping genealogy patrons as well as from genealogy librarians. It centers on topics of mutual interest, but it does not accept questions on locating ancestors.

Roots-L

To subscribe, send an e-mail to ROOTS-L-request@rootsweb.com, with *subscribe* as the only word in the body of the message. This is the largest of the mailing lists for genealogy. You can choose either to receive each message as it comes or in digest format, where messages are grouped giving subject. There are many files and databases as offshoots from this one. Mainly pertains to the United States.

World Wide Web Addresses

Barrel of Genealogy Links
http://cpcug.org/user/jlacombe/mark.html

> Another site with lots and lots of links to other sites. Many links to Civil War resources, tips on how to use search engines, family oriented sites, commercial sites, and more.

College of Arms, London
http://www.kwtelecom.com/heraldry/collarms/

> For matters of heraldry and coats of arms, this is the place.

Cyndi's List of Genealogy Sites
http://www.cyndislist.com

> One of the larger lists of sites on the Internet, with well over 28,000 links in May 1998 and increasing weekly. Also one of the most current sites on the WWW, with links to about every other site imaginable for genealogical research. Judged by many to be the best site available. Divided by subject and very easy to use.

Directory of Royal Genealogy
http://www.royal.gov.uk/history/index.htm

> Anyone interested in royalty should check out this site.

Genealogy Online
http://www.genealogy.org/

> Here you will find information on genealogical societies by states in the United States and by province in Canada; international societies by countries; and family and surname associations. This can be very useful when trying to locate local information by writing to the local society for a search of its records.

Helm's Genealogy Toolbox
http://genealogy.tbox.com/

> Another site with many, many links to more information.

Journal of Online Genealogy
http://www.onlinegenealogy.com

> This free, online genealogy newsletter has lots of good tips. Subscribers are notified through e-mail of a new issue, which can be read or downloaded at the WWW address.

Library of Congress—Local History and Genealogy Reading Room
http://lcweb.loc.gov/rr/genealogy/

> Well-developed historical and informational site. You can search the Library of Congress catalogs.

Mayflower Site
http://members.aol.com/calebj/mayflower.html

> An excellent example of what a web site should be. All passengers of the *Mayflower* are listed with biographical information on each. What is really outstanding is the author of the site has included references to where he documented his sources of information.

National Archives and Records Administration
http://www.nara.gov/

> Excellent site for searching the holdings of the National Archives. Most of its finding aids are searchable from here—a good way to prepare for a visit to Washington.

Olive Tree Genealogy Homepage
http://www.rootsweb.com/~ote

> Group of detailed information sites, with lots of links to ships lists, Tools & Tips, Mennonites, the Dutch in New York, and more.

Rand Genealogy Club
http://www.rand.org/personal/genea/

> Filled with links to many sites and useful documents, organized by regional, ethnic, and religious groups. Good site with historical information, a Soundex converter (which automatically converts a surname into Soundex code—see section 4, on censuses), and lots of information on how to get started doing genealogical research, how to research, and more.

Repositories of Primary Sources
http://www.uidaho.edu/special-collections/Other.Repositories.html

> This leads to worldwide sources that describe holdings of manuscripts, archives, rare books, historical photographs, and so forth. Provides links to other sites.

Social Security Death Index
http://www.ancestry.com/ssdi/advanced.htm

> With the basic information of name and Social Security number, this site will check the Social Security Index (SSI). The Death Index lists only those persons whose death benefits were paid to survivors, not everyone who had a Social Security number.

Society of Genealogists, London, United Kingdom
http://www.sog.org.uk

> This is the best known society in the United Kingdom and probably has the best collection as well.

Treasure Maps

http://www.firstct.com/fo/tmapmenu.html

> Excellent site for those starting out in genealogy as well as for those more advanced. Lots of tips and good advice. This is a free newsletter and well worth adding to your list of items to check monthly.

U.S. Gen Web

http://www.usgenweb.com/

> This is a very easy site to use as it has lists by state. Entries for all states are consistent. Each state has a listing by county and from there to the society. These listings give information on societies' holdings, charges for mail queries, dues, meetings, information on joining the societies, what publications they have, and so forth.

Vital Records Information

http://www.inlink.com/~nomi/vitalrec/staterec.html

> Lists addresses for vital records for every state in the union, plus U.S. territories abroad. Each state listing has information on records' availability, cost for various types of records, and addresses for many county and town record offices as well.

SECTION 17

Genealogical Periodicals

This list of periodicals covers the nationally known titles, which are the basis of most large collections. In addition, almost every society publishes a newsletter or another journal. Check the societies in your area, and try to obtain a copy for your collection. This type of publication usually relates to the county, state, or area of the society; and in these publications many of the early records are published, such as vital records, cemetery readings, abstracts and inventories of wills, lists of militia, and so forth.

The American Genealogist (TAG) 1937–.
P.O. Box 398
Demorest, GA 30535
(706) 865-6440
Subscription price: $25 per year (four issues)

> Focus is on critical problem-solving articles and short compiled genealogies. One of the most respected journals in the field.

Ancestry
Ancestry.com, 1982–.
P.O. Box 476
Salt Lake City, UT 84110-0476
(800) 531-1790
Subscription price: $24.95 per year (six issues)

> Excellent little journal that gives great hints for helping with genealogical research.

Everton's Genealogical Helper
Everton Publishers, 1947–.
P.O. Box 368
Logan, UT 84323-0368
(435) 752-6022
E-mail: bob@everton.com
Subscription price: $24 per year

> Everton Publishers also had an online version of this title but suspended publication at the end of 1997. Back issues can be found at http://www.everton.com/b2.htm. Lots of basic tips for getting started.

Family Chronicle

P.O. Box 1201
Lewiston, NY 14092-9934
E-mail: magazine@familychronicle.com
Subscription price: $21 per year (six issues)

This journal began with the September/October 1996 issue and is one of the best general genealogical publications on the market. Covers such topics as preservation of papers and photographs, ethnic research tips, web sites worth searching, new genealogy programs, and so on.

Genealogy Bulletin

American Genealogical Lending Library
593 W. 100 N
P.O. Box 329
Bountiful, UT 84011-0329
Nonmember subscription price: $18 per year (six issues)

Has articles, reviews, advertising, and news items on the latest in genealogy.

Genealogy Computing

Ancestry.com, 1981–.
266 W. Center Street
Orem, UT 84057
Subscription price: $25 per year (four issues)

Covers the world of computing as it relates to genealogy.

Heritage Quest

Heritage Quest International Genealogy Forum, 1985–.
P.O. Box 329
Bountiful, UT 84011-0329
Subscription price: $28 per year

Another title that is very good for how-to articles, lots of ads for genealogical help, lists of libraries, and so forth.

National Genealogical Society Quarterly

National Genealogical Society, 1912–.
4527 17th Street N
Arlington, VA 22207-2399
(703) 525-0050
FAX: (703) 525-0052

Comes with membership as well as the *NGS Newsletter,* which includes the *NGS/CIG Digest.*

New England Historical and Genealogical Register

New England Historical and Genealogical Society, 1847–.
101 Newbury Street
Boston, MA 02116
(800) 296-6687
FAX: (410) 752-8492

Subscription price: $40 per year (four issues and includes *Nexus,* a bimonthly publication)

This is one of the oldest continuing publications on genealogy.

New York Genealogical and Biographical Record
New York Genealogical and Biographical Society, 1870–.
122 E. 58th Street, Suite 305
New York, NY 10022-1939
(212) 755-8532
FAX: (212) 754-4218
Subscription price: $25 per year (four issues)

Excellent source for New York families, especially in the Hudson Valley, Long Island, and New York City areas.

Periodical Source Index (PERSI)
Allen County Public Library, Genealogy Section
900 Webster Street
Fort Wayne, IN 46802

This is a subject index to genealogy and local history periodicals, with about 5,000 titles since 1800. In print form, it is 27 volumes and costs $2,000. It came out in CD-ROM form in 1997 at a cost of $99.95 by Ancestry.com, in Orem, Utah, and has five sections.

1. Specific families (440,162 entries)
2. Canada and Canadian peoples (21,510 entries)
3. The United States and U.S. peoples (547,680 entries)
4. Lands and peoples outside the U.S. and Canada (40,077 entries)
5. Genealogy methods and skills (18,193 entries)

Add other titles here as desired.

English Genealogy, Regnal Years, and the Change in Calendar

In older documents in England, dates are often given in *regnal years*. This relates to the years of the reign of various monarchs in England, and you must know the dates of the reigns of the various monarchs to interpret regnal years. For example, a will might refer to a death on the fifth day of June in the tenth year of the reign of our Gracious Queen Elizabeth I. Once you know the dates of the various reigns, you can interpret the exact date. The regnal year begins with the first date of the reign—for Elizabeth I, her reign began on 17 November 1558. Therefore, the fifth day of June in the tenth year of her reign would be 05 June 1568. The various regnal dates follow.

William I	25 Dec 1066	Henry VII	22 Aug 1485
William II	26 Sep 1087	Henry VIII	22 Apr 1509
Henry I	05 Aug 1100	Edward VI	28 Jan 1547
Stephen	26 Dec 1135	Mary	06 Jul 1553
Henry II	19 Dec 1154	Philip & Mary	25 Jul 1554
Richard I	03 Sep 1189	Elizabeth I	17 Nov 1558
John*	27 May 1199	James I†	24 Mar 1603
Henry III	28 Oct 1216	Charles I	27 Mar 1625
Edward I	20 Nov 1272	Commonwealth‡	
Edward II	08 Jul 1307	Charles II	30 Jan 1649
Edward III	25 Jan 1327	James II	06 Feb 1685
Richard II	22 Jun 1377	Interregnum	12 Dec 1688
Henry IV	30 Sep 1399	to	12 Feb 1689
Henry V	21 Mar 1413	William III	
Henry VI	01 Sep 1422	and Mary	13 Feb 1689
Edward IV	04 Mar 1461	William III	28 Dec 1694
Edward V	09 Apr 1483	Anne	08 Mar 1702
Richard III	26 Jun 1483	George I	01 Aug 1714

George II	11 Jun 1727	William IV	26 Jun 1830
George III	25 Oct 1760	Victoria	20 Jun 1837
George IV	29 Jan 1820	(regnal years discontinued)	

---

*Regnal years are calculated from Ascension Day each year, and each year this date is different as Ascension Day changes with the religious calendar.

†James I is also known as James VI of Scotland.

‡During the Commonwealth, there were no regnal years as such. At the Restoration, on 9 May 1660, the years of Charles II were backdated to the death of Charles I, as he was designated in principle as being king from that date.

For further information on this interesting way of dating documents, check Angus Baxter's *In Search of Your British and Irish Roots* (Baltimore, Md.: Genealogical Publishing Co., 1987); and David Hey's *Oxford Dictionary of Local and Family History* (Oxford: Oxford University Press, 1997). The British Royal Family web page (http://www.royal.gov.uk) also lists the reigns of all the monarchs but without explanation. There is a computer program, British Date Calculator Version 1.0, that will compute dates for you. Check http://www.tdrake.demon.co.uk/datecal2.htm. The program sells for about $12.

Another fact that must be considered when using dates is the change in the calendar in 1752 from the Julian calendar (old style) to the Gregorian calendar (new style). In addition to that change, the year now began on 01 January instead of 25 March. All this change caused a loss of eleven days and resulted in many a riot by the people wanting their eleven days back. For further information on the calendar change, consult *Encyclopedia Britannica*, or any other good encyclopedia, or how-to books on English genealogy. Various countries made the change at different times, something else to consider when working with older dates. You will see many dates listed as 1665/6, for example, and this must be noted as such in record keeping. This designation is for the years of the calendar change. The British Date Calculator computer program, mentioned earlier, will compute dates from both the Julian and the Gregorian calendar.

Military Service Records and American Wars and Engagements, 1565–1990

MILITARY SERVICE RECORDS

Military service records have been created in times of peace as well as war, at a local, state, or federal level. To locate and use these records, some basic information is needed. You must know whether the person was an enlistee or an officer, when and where this person served in the military, and what unit he or she served in.

During the colonial period, local governments required all able-bodied men between the ages of sixteen and sixty to join the militia. This is the oldest military organization in the United States and provides one of the longest ongoing systems of records available. The men were expected to provide their own weapons and ammunition and to report regularly for scheduled drills. They could be fined for missing drills, and this type of record could be found in the town minutes. They were prepared to face marauding Native Americans, pirates, criminals, and foreign adventurers, depending on the area. The militia continued into the formation of the Union and is noted in the Constitution as necessary for the security of the people. Local militia continued to exist until 1903, when federal status was given, and the units became known as the National Guard.

The following gives some idea of the types of military service records and what they cover.

Definitions of Terms and Types of Military Service Records

Compiled Military Service Record—abstracts of information found on original documents reflecting the military service of individuals. This reflects all data found on all the original records relating to each individual's service.

Enlistment Register—document prepared at the time of enlistment setting forth the term of service and conditions. Some personal data appears here.

Muster Roll—report listing the names, ranks, and other data about persons assigned to a particular military unit, giving cause for any absences, sick call, and so forth.

Pension—payments received after completion of required term of service or to the qualified survivors of servicemen or servicewomen.

Regulars—persons who served in the permanent military forces such as the U.S. Army, Navy, Marine Corps, Coast Guard, and Air Force, both in wartime or peacetime.

Return—report containing only the names of the officers assigned to the unit and giving statistical data about other persons in the unit as well.

Volunteer—persons serving during wartime, whether or not of their own volition.

Militia records will be found in the town or state records depending on the date and whether the unit was a town or state unit. Many genealogical societies and state agencies have preserved these records and published them in journals or books. Consult *PERSI* (see section 17) for periodical articles or *Genealogical and Local Books in Print* to locate militia records for your area and state.

There are two types of records for the federal military units. One is the enlistment, or service, record, which chronicles the day-to-day activity of the soldier, when he or she enlisted, was transferred, was on sick call, was promoted, reported for duty, and so forth. Enlistment records are interesting to have but do not provide the genealogical information desired. The pension records are the most fruitful for genealogists and can include a wealth of information. It is not uncommon to find letters home, diaries, birth certificates, divorce records, and many other types of records.

This is especially true if a widowed spouse, mother, or other family member is trying to claim the pension. The National Archives has the pension records there. You can also write for copies, but you must know whether the person was an enlistee or an officer, when and where this person served in the military, and in which unit he or she served. The form number is 80 (see appendix 18). Be sure to state pension records or compiled service records to obtain the complete record. Do not send any money as the National Archives will search for the records you request, and if the records are found, the archives will send you a bill for the dollar amount needed for photocopies. After your check is received, the records will be copied and sent.

AMERICAN WARS AND ENGAGEMENTS, 1565–1990

Most American history books give details on many or all of the following wars as well as many engagements not included here. As noted in the following list, the United States has had a history of one uprising, war, or another since the country was settled. Thus, there is a voluminous collection of records, enlistment forms, pension records, and muster rolls. These records can contain detailed personal information such as date of birth, place of residence, loved ones at home, and more.

War	Dates	Area
French-Spanish	1565–67	Florida
Jamestown Conflicts	1622–44	Virginia
Anglo-French War	1629	St. Lawrence River
Pequot War	1636–37	Connecticut
Dutch and Indian Skirmishes	1640–45	New Netherland
Iroquois	1642–53	New England
Bacon's Rebellion	1675–76	Virginia
King Philip's	1675–76	Massachusetts, Rhode Island
Culpepper's Rebellion	1677–80	The Carolinas
Revolution in Maryland	1689	Maryland
King William's War	1689–97	New England, New York
Queen Anne's	1702–13	Massachusetts, South Carolina, Florida
Yamasee War	1715–16	South Carolina, Georgia
Jenkin's Ear	1739–42	Georgia, Florida
King George's War	1740–48	New England, New York
French and Indian War	1754–63	Northern colonies
Siege of Quebec	1759	Canada
Cherokee Uprising	1760–61	The Carolinas
Pontiac's Rebellion	1763	Michigan, New York, Pennsylvania
War of the Regulators	1771	North Carolina
Lord Dunmore's War	1774	Virginia, Pennsylvania, Ohio
American Revolution	1775–83	American colonies
Shay's Rebellion	1786–87	Massachusetts
Whiskey Rebellion	1794	Pennsylvania
War with France	1798–1800	Atlantic Coast, West Indies
Barbary Wars	1801–5	North Africa
Burr's Insurrection	1806–7	South Mississippi Valley
War of 1812	1812–15	District of Columbia, Maryland, New Orleans
Indian Wars	1811–58	United States and Territories
1st Seminole War	1817–19	Florida
Black Hawk War	1831–32	Illinois, Wisconsin
2d Seminole War	1835–42	Florida
War of Texas Independence	1836	Texas
Creek Indian Wars	1836–37	Georgia, Alabama
Aroostook War	1839	Maine
Dorr Rebellion	1841	Rhode Island
Mexican War	1846–48	Texas, New Mexico, California

Navajo Wars	1846–68	New Mexico, Arizona
3d Seminole War	1848–58	Florida
Utah (Mormon)	1857–58	Utah
American Civil War	1861–65	The South, border states, Pennsylvania
Indian Wars	1865–1900	Western states
Sioux & Cheyenne	1866–90	The Dakotas, Montana
Apache Wars	1870–86	Arizona, New Mexico, Mexico
Modoc War	1872–73	California
Nez Percé Wars	1877	Idaho, Montana
Spanish-American War	1898	Cuba, Philippine Islands
Philippine Insurrection	1899–1902	Philippine Islands
Boxer Rebellion	1900	China
World War I	1914–19	Europe
World War II	1939–1945	Europe, Africa, the Pacific
Korean War	1950–53	Korea
Vietnam War	1955–1975	Vietnam
Gulf War	1990	Saudia Arabia, Kuwait

There are extensive bibliographies on the military engagements from the colonial time to the present. Two books of note that deal with the genealogical aspects of military records follow: James C. Neagles, *U.S. Military Records: A Guide to Federal and State Sources, Colonial America to the Present* (Salt Lake City, Utah: Ancestry, 1994) and *Military Service Records: A Select Catalog of National Archives Microfilm Publications* (Washington, D.C.: National Archives and Records Administration, 1985). The latter details where the records are located in the National Archives and how you can access them. These records are on microfilm and list the Record Group (RG), the microfilm reel number, by state, company, regiment, and date. They include volunteers, regular army, veterans' claims, and miscellaneous records such as those pertaining to military academy cadets and naval academy midshipmen. Veterans' claims include Revolutionary War Bounty Land Warrant Applications and Pensions, War of 1812 Bounty Land Warrants, and pensions and other veterans' claims.

A sampling of other titles that deal with the military follow.

Bunnell, Paul J. *Research Guide to Loyalist Ancestors: A Directory to Archives, Manuscripts, and Published Sources.* Bowie, Md.: Heritage Books, 1990.

Coldham, Peter W. *American Loyalist Claims: Abstracted from the Public Record Office.* Audit Office Series 13. Washington, D.C.: National Genealogical Society, 1976.

MacGregor, Morris J., ed. *Blacks in the United States Armed Forces, Basic Documents.* 13 vols. Wilmington, Del.: Scholarly Resources, 1977. Volume 1 covers the colonial era.

Civil War Soldiers and Sailors System is an online system being developed by the cooperation of the National Park Service, the Federation of Genealogical Societies, the Genealogical Society of Utah, and the United Daughters of the

Confederacy. It is hoped eventually to list every name of every serviceman, with his rank and regimental unit, whether Union or Confederate. The uniform resource locator (URL) is http://www.itd.nps.gov/cwss/. Some names are available for searching now, and eventually every National Park will have this capability for this searching on a computer.

Heitman, Francis B. *Historical Register and Dictionary of the United States Army: From Its Organization, Sept. 29, 1789 to March 2, 1903.* 2 vols. Urbana: University of Illinois Press, 1965.

Index of Revolutionary War Pension Applications in the National Archives. Special Publication No. 40. Washington, D.C.: National Genealogical Society, 1976.

Official Records of the Union and Confederate Armies. War of the Rebellion. Washington, D.C.: GPO, 1880–1900.

Official Records of the Union and Confederate Navies. War of the Rebellion. Washington, D.C.: GPO, 1894–1927.

Miscellaneous Tidbits

FRATERNAL ORGANIZATIONS

Most of these groups will do a limited search if you know the exact location of the chapter and the time frame. Many tombstones will have some symbol denoting in which organization the deceased was a member. There are probably some branches of one or more of these groups in your area. If so, try to locate their addresses and contact persons and add here.

American Legion National Headquarters
P.O. Box 1055
700 N. Pennsylvania Street
Indianapolis, IN 46206
(317) 630-1200
FAX: (317) 630-1223
http://www.legion.org/

Ancient Accepted Scottish Rite of Free Masonry (Masons)
1733 16th Street NW
Washington, DC 20009-3103
http://www.srmason-sj.org/

Benevolent and Protective Order of Elks (BPOE)
2750 N. Lakeview Avenue
Chicago, IL 60614-1889
(773) 477-2750
E-mail: grandlodge@elks.org
http://www.elks.org

Fraternal Order of the Eagles (FOE)
P.O. Box 25916
Milwaukee, WI 53225-0916
(414) 781-7585
FAX: (414) 781-5046

Imperial Council of the Ancient Arabic Order of the Nobles of the Mystic Shrine for North America (Shriners)
P.O. Box 31356
Tampa, FL 33631-3356
(813) 281-0300
FAX: (813) 281-8174

Great Council of U.S. Improved Order of Red Men
4521 Speight Avenue
Waco, TX 76711-1708
(817) 756-1221
FAX: (817) 756-4828
E-mail: redmen@iamerica.com

Independent Order of Odd Fellows (IOOF)
Sovereign Grand Lodge IOOF
16 W. Chase Street
Baltimore, MD 21201
(336) 725-5955
(800) 235-8358
FAX: (336) 722-7317
http://norm28.hsc.usc.edu/IOOF.html

Knights of Columbus (K of C)
Columbus Plaza
New Haven, CT 06510-3326
(203) 772-2130
FAX: (203) 773-3000

Loyal Order of Moose
Route 31
Mooseheart, IL 60539
(630) 859-2000
FAX: (630) 859-6618

Supreme Lodge, Knights of Pythias
1495 Hancock Street
Quincy, MA 02169
(617) 472-8800
FAX: (617) 376-0363
E-mail: kon@earthlink.net

Woodmen of the World (WOW)
Woodman Tower, 1700 Farnam Street
Omaha, NE 68102
(800) 225-3108
E-mail: service@woodmen.com

> Founded in 1890, in Omaha, Nebraska. It was one of the first fraternal benefit societies in the United States, designed for fraternalism, protection, and

service. Strong in patriotic sentiments, Woodmen have some 2,600 lodges around the country, and one of their strongest programs is the presentation of American flags to civic and community organizations.

LINEAGE SOCIETIES

There are more than one hundred lineage, patriotic, and veterans societies that one can join if all requirements of heredity are met. The following is only a partial listing showing the variety of the societies with some of the requirements needed for membership. Check Robert R. Davenport, ed., *Hereditary Society Blue Book* (Baltimore, Md.: Genealogical Publishing Co., 1994) for a more complete listing.

Ancient and Honorable Artillery Company of Massachusetts
Armory, Faneuil Hall
Boston, MA 02109
(617) 227-1638
FAX: (617) 227-7221

Limited to males who can prove they are direct descendants of a former member of the company whose service dated prior to 1738.

Associated Daughters of Early American Witches
Mrs. William Alfred Smith
850-A Thornhill Court
Lakewood, NJ 08701

Females must be at least sixteen years of age and can prove descent from an ancestor who was accused, tried, or executed for practice of witchcraft prior to 31 December 1699.

Baronial Order of the Magna Charta
625 S. Bethlehem Pike
Ambler, PA 19002
(215) 628-2349

Must prove lineal descent from one or more of the twenty-four barons and the Lord Mayor of London who were selected to be sureties for the proper observance of the Magna Charta in 1215. Women were admitted in 1992.

Colonial Dames of America
421 E. 61st Street
New York, NY 10021
(212) 838-5489

Women must be eighteen years of age and able to prove descent from an ancestor beginning with the settlement of Jamestown, Virginia, 13 May 1607 to the Battle of Lexington, 19 April 1775.

Daughters of Union Veterans of the Civil War, 1861–1865
503 S. Walnut Street
Springfield, IL 62704
(217) 544-0616

> Limited to women who can prove lineal descent of soldiers and sailors
> who served between 12 April 1861 and 9 April 1865.

Descendants of the Illegitimate Sons and Daughters of the Kings of Britain
3502 N. Oakley Avenue
Chicago, IL 60618

> Descent must be proved from an illegitimate son or daughter of a king of
> England, Scotland, or Wales.

Flagon and Trencher
Mrs. William Alfred Smith
850-A Thornhill Court
Lakewood, NJ 08701-6661
(908) 920-3279

> Limited to persons who can provide genealogical proof of direct descent
> from an ancestor who operated a tavern, ordinary, inn, or other type of
> hostelry prior to 4 July 1776.

General Society of Mayflower Descendants
Mayflower Society House
4 Winslow Street
P.O. Box 3297
Plymouth, MA 02360
(508) 746-3188

> Must be eighteen years of age or older and prove descent from one of the
> passengers on the *Mayflower*.

Huguenot Society of America
122 E. 58th Street
New York, NY 10022
(212) 755-0592

> Must be eighteen years of age, Protestant religion, and prove descent in
> male or female line of a Huguenot émigré from France prior to the Edict of
> Toleration, 28 November 1787.

National Society Children of the American Revolution (NSCAR)
1776 D Street NW
Washington, DC 20006
(202) 638-3153

> Must be under twenty-one years of age, boy or girl, who can prove
> descent from man or woman who rendered material aid and served as
> soldier, sailor, or otherwise proved loyalty to the cause of American inde-
> pendence.

National Society Daughters of Founders and Patriots of America
Park Lane Building, Suites 300–305
2025 I Street NW
Washington, DC 20006
(202) 833-1558

> Female must be at least eighteen years of age and descend in unbroken male line, either father or mother line, who settled in one of the colonies from 13 May 1607 to 13 May 1687 and also had an ancestor in this unbroken line who rendered assistance in the American Revolution, 1774–1784.

National Society Daughters of the American Revolution (DAR)
1776 D Street NW
Washington, DC 20006-5392
(202) 628-1776
http://www.dar.org

> Must document line back to the ancestor who either served in the Revolution or gave material aid to the cause.

National Society of the Colonial Dames of America
Dumbarton House
2715 Q Street NW
Washington, DC 20007
(202) 337-2288

> Women of lineal descent from an ancestor who resided in an American colony prior to 1750 and who served in an important capacity to the colony and contributed to the founding of the United States.

National Society of the Sons of the American Revolution (SAR)
1000 S. 4th Street
Louisville, KY 40203
(502) 589-1776
http://www.sar.org/

> Any man over eighteen years of age who can prove his descent from one who served in the cause of American independence and was recognized as a patriot.

Society of the Cincinnati
2118 Massachusetts Avenue NW
Washington, DC 20008
(202) 785-2040

> Must prove descent from an officer in the Continental Army or Navy who served in the French forces under Rochambeau or DeGrass. Hereditary membership includes the eldest male in each generation.

GENERAL SOURCES

Association for Gravestone Studies
278 Main Street, Suite 207
Greenfield, MA 01301
(413) 772-0836
E-mail: ags@javanet.com
http://www.berkshire.net/ags/

For questions on preservation of gravestones, how to do a rubbing without harming the stone, or any others that arise on this subject, they are the experts. They publish a journal called *Markers: Journal of the Association for Gravestone Studies.* Their journal is quite fascinating reading and full of tidbits on the older stones in the older graveyards. There are other books about this subject, such as Lynette Sangstad's *Graveyard Preservation Primer* (Walnut Creek, Calif.: AlataMira Press, 1995). This deals with the preservation of graveyards and can be used by professionals or nonprofessionals alike. Covers such topics as landscaping, stone restoration, and carvers and includes a glossary and a list of sources for further information. Another book, which is more for fun reading, is Janet Greene's *Epitaphs to Remember: Remarkable Inscriptions from New England* (Brattleboro, Vt.: Alan C. Hood and Co., 1996). This makes for lots of laughs at what some of our ancestors had carved on their stones for posterity.

Circus Workers

Florida: The John and Mable Ringling
    Museum of Art
5401 Bay Shore Road
P.O. Box 1838
Sarasota, FL 34243
(941) 359-5700
FAX: (941) 359-5745
http://www.ringling.org

Ohio: Circus Historical Society
800 Ritchy Road
Zanesville, OH 43701

Pennsylvania: Circus Fans Association
    of Ameria
P.O. Box 59710
Potomac, MD 20859
(301) 762-8272

Wisconsin: Library and Research
    of Circus World
415 Lynn Street
Baraboo, WI 53913

Erie Canal Workers

The Canal Museum   or
Weighlock Building
Erie Boulevard E
Syracuse, NY 13202

New York State Archives
11040 Cultural Education Center,
    Room 11040
Empire State Plaza
Albany, NY 12230
(518) 474-8955

For any ancestor who possibly worked on the building of the Erie Canal, send a self-addressed, stamped envelope (SASE) requesting a search of their records. Be sure to include full name, possible location, and dates if known or suspected.

Marine Historical Association, Mystic Seaport Museum,
G. W. Blunt White Library
Greenmanville Avenue
P.O. Box 6000
Mystic, CT 06355-0990
(860) 572-5367
FAX: (860) 572-5394
http://www.mystic.org/public/library/blunt.library.html

This is a reconstructed village built around sea life—a marvelous place to visit to get a feel of what life on the sea was like in the days of sailing ships. You can experience everything about sail making, go aboard a sailing ship, see ship carvers at work, view costumes of a sailor, and visit the museum to see the wares the ships brought back. The library is a research library, and as such there are restrictions for use. Do not let that deter you from making use of its records, which include charts, maps, periodicals, a union list of logbooks and journals, and a ship's register room, where you will find a very extensive collection of aids for identifying American vessels.

Mariners' Museum Research Library and Archives
100 Museum Drive
Newport News, VA 23606
(804) 595-0368
http://mariner.org

The sea played a very important part in the life of our ancestors, whether they were on the *Mayflower* or any of the immigrant ships in the nineteenth century. This is not only a great museum for ship models, figureheads of ships, scrimshaw, or any of the other items associated with shipping—it also has a great collection of pictures of ships. I was able to obtain copies of pictures of the ships an ancestor captained while he traveled the seas. If you know the name of the ship an ancestor traveled on to come to the United States, write to this library and archives to check for particulars. The museum is a fascinating place to visit, and it would be worthwhile to write for any brochures or visit its web site for particulars.

National Genealogical Society
Attn.: AMA Research
4527 17th Street N
Arlington, VA 22207-2399

The National Genealogical Society now has the records of the American Medical Association (AMA) of deceased American physicians. At present, the holdings are incomplete from 1878 to 1905 but comprehensive from 1906 to 1969. The earlier cards have little information other than medical school attended and date of graduation. The later cards are quite comprehensive and can give lots of genealogical information. You must send first and last name of the physician, time period, and location if possible. There is a $15 research fee, prepayment required. Surnames from *A* through *L* are available now; the rest of the alphabet will be available in a few months.

National Personnel Records Center

9700 Page Boulevard
St. Louis, MO 63132-5100

> The principal service of this center is to provide proof of service and re-
> lated military data to servicemen and -women and, if deceased, to their
> next of kin. There are no research facilities at this center. A fire in 1973 de-
> stroyed a large portion of the U.S. Army and Air Force records for person-
> nel who served in World War I and II and the Korean War, but many of
> these records have been re-created from other sources. It is always worth a
> request to see what is available. The NARA Southeast Region Branch, at
> East Point, Georgia, houses the draft records for World War I, and various
> regional branches also have military records.

Salvation Army

National Headquarters
615 Slaters Lane
P.O. Box 269
Alexandria, VA 22313
(703) 684-5500
FAX: (703) 684-3478

> The Salvation Army will do a search for a living missing member of the
> immediate family only. This is limited to persons age eighteen and older.
> There is a $25 fee, nonrefundable.

Social Security Administration

Freedom of Information Officer
4-H-8 Annex Building
6401 Security Boulevard
Baltimore, MD 21235
(401) 965-7700

> Under the Freedom of Information Act, you can write to the department re-
> questing a photocopy of the application for Social Security number of a de-
> ceased ancestor. You will need to send the Social Security number, full
> name, full name at birth, date of birth, and sex. It also is necessary to state
> the relationship to the deceased, and if you have a copy of the death certifi-
> cate, send a photocopy of that for quicker service. Be patient, as it could
> take several weeks before you receive a reply. The charge for this service is
> $7 if the Social Security number is known, $16.50 if the number is unknown.

Steamship Historical Society of America (SSHSA)

University of Baltimore
1420 Maryland Avenue
Baltimore, MD 21201
(410) 625-3134
http://sshsa.org/index.html

> This society has a library at the University of Baltimore Library: the SSHSA
> Collection, 1420 Maryland Avenue, Baltimore, MD 21201. Also the South
> Street Seaport Museum Library, 213 Water Street, New York NY 10038, is
> another location for information on ships and seamen.

United States Army Military History Institute
Carlisle Barracks
PA 17013-5008
(717) 245-3611

> This center collects, preserves, and makes available to researchers source material pertaining to American military history. There are three principal sections: reference, manuscripts, and photographs. This would be the place to go for photographs of various military units from the Civil War to date. Other branches of the military have their own research facilities as well. Consult James C. Neagles, *U.S. Military Records: A Guide to Federal and State Sources, Colonial America to the Present* (Salt Lake City, Utah: Ancestry, 1994), for addresses.

United States Railroad Retirement Board
Office of Public Affairs
844 N. Rush Street
Chicago, IL 60611-2092
(800) 808-0772
http://www.rrb.gov

> This is the place to write for railroad personnel who retired after 1936. This board was established in the mid-1930s and is patterned after the Social Security Administration. Send $16 for each individual for whom records are requested, and make checks payable to the Railroad Retirement Board. This is a nonrefundable fee whether information is located or not. You will need the Social Security number of the employee for a better chance of locating the records, as well as the full name, including middle initial, and complete dates of birth and death. The board can not locate inactive records by names of spouses or widowed spouses.

Appendixes

1. Research Calendar

Date	Surname	Source Searched/ Source Location	What Found

2. Correspondence Calendar

Date	Address	Information Requested	Information Received	Amount Sent

3. Ancestor Chart

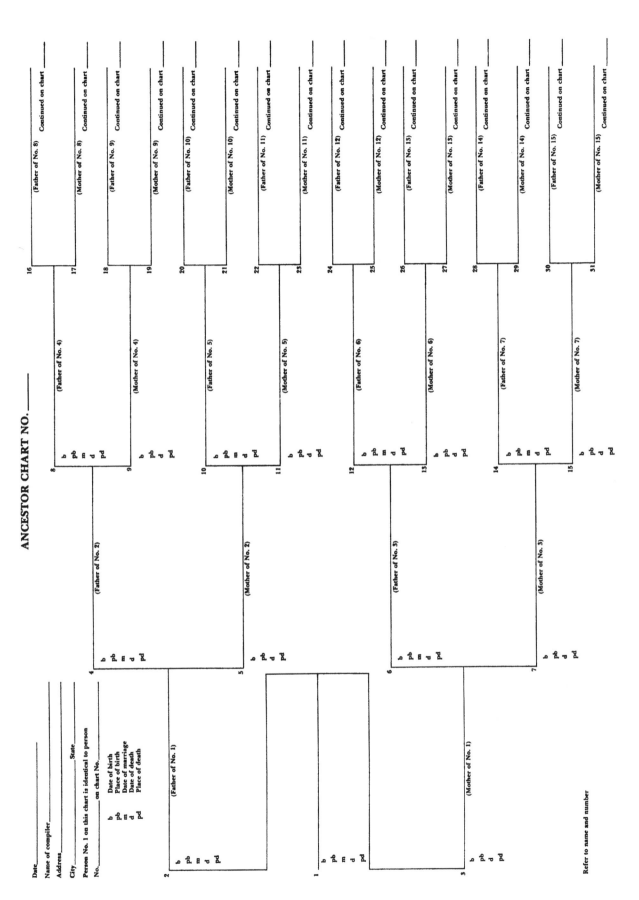

ANCESTOR CHART NO._____

Date_____
Name of compiler_____
Address_____
City_____ State_____
Person No. 1 on this chart is identical to person
No._____ on chart No._____

b   Date of birth
pb   Place of birth
m   Date of marriage
d   Date of death
pd   Place of death

(Father of No. 1)
(Mother of No. 1)
(Father of No. 2)
(Mother of No. 2)
(Father of No. 3)
(Mother of No. 3)
(Father of No. 4)
(Mother of No. 4)
(Father of No. 5)
(Mother of No. 5)
(Father of No. 6)
(Mother of No. 6)
(Father of No. 7)
(Mother of No. 7)

(Father of No. 8)   Continued on chart_____
(Mother of No. 8)   Continued on chart_____
(Father of No. 9)   Continued on chart_____
(Mother of No. 9)   Continued on chart_____
(Father of No. 10)   Continued on chart_____
(Mother of No. 10)   Continued on chart_____
(Father of No. 11)   Continued on chart_____
(Mother of No. 11)   Continued on chart_____
(Father of No. 12)   Continued on chart_____
(Mother of No. 12)   Continued on chart_____
(Father of No. 13)   Continued on chart_____
(Mother of No. 13)   Continued on chart_____
(Father of No. 14)   Continued on chart_____
(Mother of No. 14)   Continued on chart_____
(Father of No. 15)   Continued on chart_____
(Mother of No. 15)   Continued on chart_____

Refer to name and number

105

4. Family Group Record

Wife		Husband		
	Name			
		Born		
		Married		
		Died		
		Burial		
	Father			
	Mother			
Husband	Other (If Any)	Wife		

Notes

Date Married & Spouse

#	Sex	Children in Order of Birth	Born Day Month Year	Where Born	Died Day Month Year	Where Died

Source	By

107

5. 1800–1810 Census—United States

State _____ County _____ City _____ Call No. _____

Page	Head of Family	Free White Males					Free White Females					All Others	Slaves	Remarks
		Under 10	10–16	16–26	26–45	45 & Over	Under 10	10–16	16–26	26–45	45 & Over			

6. 1820 Census—United States

State _____ County _____ City _____ Call No. _____

Page	Head of Family	Free White Males						Free White Females					Foreigners not naturalized	Agriculture	Commerce	Manufactures	Free Colored	Slaves	Remarks
		Under 10	10–16	16–18	18–26	26–45	45 & Over	Under 10	10–16	16–26	26–45	45 & Over							

7. 1830–1840 Census—United States

STATE	COUNTY	CITY	CALL NUMBER

HEAD OF FAMILY	Page		FREE WHITE MALES													FREE WHITE FEMALES														Slaves	Free Colored	Foreigners Not Naturalized
			Under 5	5–10	10–15	15–20	20–30	30–40	40–50	50–60	60–70	70–80	80–90	90–100	Over 100	Under 5	5–10	10–15	15–20	20–30	30–40	40–50	50–60	60–70	70–80	80–90	90–100	Over 100			

NA 14082 (10-88)

NATIONAL ARCHIVES AND RECORDS ADMINISTRATION

113

8. 1850 Census—United States

STATE		COUNTY				TOWN/TOWNSHIP						CALL NUMBER		
Page	Dwelling Number	Family Number	NAMES	Age	Sex	Color	OCCUPATION, ETC.	Value—Real Estate	BIRTHPLACE	Married Within Year	School Within Year	Can't Read or Write	Enumeration Date	REMARKS

NATIONAL ARCHIVES AND RECORDS ADMINISTRATION   *U.S. Government Printing Office: 1989-235-091/00030   NA 14083 (10-88)

9. 1860 Census—United States

STATE	COUNTY	TOWN/TOWNSHIP	P.O.	CALL NUMBER

Page	Dwelling No.	Family No.	NAMES	Age	Sex	Color	OCCUPATION, ETC.	Value—Real Estate	Value—Personal Property	BIRTHPLACE	Married In Year	School In Year	Can't Read or Write	Enumeration Date	REMARKS

NA 14084 (10-88)

*U.S. GPO: 1993-342-619/83329

NATIONAL ARCHIVES AND RECORDS ADMINISTRATION

10. 1870 Census—United States

STATE	COUNTY	TOWN/TOWNSHIP	P.O.	CALL NUMBER

Page	Dwelling No.	Family No.	NAMES	Age	Sex	Color	OCCUPATION, ETC.	Value—Real Estate	Value—Personal Property	BIRTHPLACE	Father Foreign Born	Mother Foreign Born	Month Born In Year	Month Married in Year	School In Year	Can't Read or Write	Eligible To Vote	Date of Enumeration

NA 14085 (10-88)

*U.S. GPO: 1993-342-619/83329

NATIONAL ARCHIVES AND RECORDS ADMINISTRATION

119

11. 1880 Census—United States

| STATE | COUNTY | TOWN/TOWNSHIP | CALL NUMBER |

Page	Dwelling Number	Family Number	NAMES	Color	Sex	Age Prior to June 1st	Month of Birth if Born in Census Year	Relationship to Head of House	Single	Married	Widowed	Divorced	Married in Census Year	Occupation	Miscellaneous Information	Cannot Read or Write	Place of Birth	Place of Birth of Father	Place of Birth of Mother	Enumeration Date

NATIONAL ARCHIVES AND RECORDS ADMINISTRATION

*U.S. GPO: 1993-342-619/83329

NA 14086 (10-88)

12. 1900 Census—United States

1900 CENSUS—UNITED STATES

MICROFILM ROLL NUMBER

STATE	TOWN/TOWNSHIP	SUPV. DIST. NO.	SHEET NUMBER
COUNTY	CALL NUMBER	ENUM. DIST. NO. DATE	PAGE NUMBER

LOCATION				NAME	PERSONAL DESCRIPTION										NATIVITY			CITIZENSHIP			OCCUPATION		EDUCATION						
Street	House Number	Dwelling Number	Family Number	of each person whose place of abode on June 1, 1900, was in this family	Relation to head of family	Color	Sex	Month of birth	Year of birth	Age	Single, married, widowed, divorced	Number of years married	Mother of how many children	Number of these children living	Place of birth	Place of birth of father	Place of birth of mother	Year of immigration to United States	No. of years in U.S.	Naturalization	Type	Number of months not employed	Attended school (months)	Can read	Can write	Can speak English	Home owned or rented	Home owned free or mortgaged	Farm or house

NA 14087 (10-88)

*U.S. GPO: 1993-342-619/83329

NATIONAL ARCHIVES AND RECORDS ADMINISTRATION

13. 1910 Census—United States

STATE		COUNTY		TOWN/TOWNSHIP										ENUM. DIST. NO.			PAGE NO.	

LOCATION				NAME	RELATION TO HEAD OF HOUSE	PERSONAL DESCRIPTION							NATIVITY		
STREET NAME	HOUSE NUMBER	VISITATION NUMBER	FAMILY NUMBER	OF EACH PERSON WHOSE PLACE OF ABODE ON APRIL 15, 1910, WAS IN THIS FAMILY		SEX	RACE	AGE	SINGLE/MARRIED/ WIDOWED/DIVORCED	NUMBER OF YEARS PRESENT MARRIAGE	NO. OF CHILDREN BORN THIS MOTHER	NUMBER OF THESE CHILDREN LIVING	PLACE OF BIRTH OF THIS PERSON	PLACE OF BIRTH OF FATHER	PLACE OF BIRTH OF MOTHER

NA 14088 (10-88)

NATIONAL ARCHIVES AND RECORDS ADMINISTRATION

125

13. 1910 Census—United States (continued)

NAME	CITIZENSHIP			OCCUPATION					EDUCATION			HOMEOWNERSHIP						
OF EACH PERSON WHOSE PLACE OF ABODE ON APRIL 15, 1910, WAS IN THIS FAMILY (FROM OTHER SIDE OF THIS FORM)	YEAR OF IMMIGRATION TO U.S.	NATURALIZED/ALIEN	NATIVE LANGUAGE	TRADE OR PROFESSION	NATURE OF BUSINESS	EMPLOYER/EMPLOYEE/ SELF-EMPLOYED	EMPLOYED/ UNEMPLOYED	WEEKS OUT OF WORK IN 1909	ABLE TO READ	ABLE TO WRITE	ATTENDED SCHOOL SINCE SEPT 1, 1909	OWNED/RENTED	OWNED FREE/ MORTGAGED	FARM/HOUSE	NO. OF FARM SCHEDULE	UNION/CONFEDERATE VETERAN	BLIND	DEAF AND DUMB

STATE ___ COUNTY ___ TOWN/TOWNSHIP ___ ENUM. DIST. NO. ___ PAGE NO. ___

IF EMPLOYEE

*U.S. Government Printing Office: 1995 — 397-951/29078

NA 14088 BACK (10-88)

14. 1920 Census—United States

1920 CENSUS — UNITED STATES

STATE

COUNTY

TOWNSHIP OR OTHER COUNTY DIVISION

NAME OF INSTITUTION

NAME OF INCORPORATED PLACE

ENUMERATED BY ME ON THE _____ DAY OF _____, 1920

SUPERVISOR'S DISTRICT #

ENUMERATION DISTRICT #

WARD OF CITY

ENUMERATOR

SHEET NO.

PLACE OF ABODE				NAME	RELATION	TENURE		PERSONAL DESCRIPTION				CITIZENSHIP			EDUCATION		
STREET, AVENUE, ETC.	HOUSE NUMBER OR FARM	NUMBER OF DWELLING HOUSE (VISITATION ORDER)	NUMBER OF FAMILY (VISITATION ORDER)	OF EACH PERSON WHOSE PLACE OF ABODE ON JANUARY 1, 1920, WAS IN THIS FAMILY	RELATIONSHIP TO HEAD OF HOUSEHOLD	HOME OWNED OR RENTED	IF OWNED, FREE OR MORTGAGED	SEX	COLOR OR RACE	AGE AT LAST BIRTHDAY	SINGLE, MARRIED WIDOWED, OR DIVORCED	YEAR OF IMMIGRATION TO U.S.	NATURALIZED OR ALIEN	IF NATURALIZED, YEAR OF NATURALIZATION	ATTENDED SCHOOL ANYTIME SINCE SEPT. 1, 1919	ABLE TO READ	ABLE TO WRITE
1	2	3	4	5	6	7	8	9	10	11	12	13	14	15	16	17	18

NA FORM 14095 (10-91)

NATIONAL ARCHIVES AND RECORDS ADMINISTRATION

1920 CENSUS — UNITED STATES

STATE		SUPERVISOR'S DISTRICT #		SHEET NO.
COUNTY		ENUMERATION DISTRICT #		
TOWNSHIP OR OTHER COUNTY DIVISION	NAME OF INCORPORATED PLACE		WARD OF CITY	
NAME OF INSTITUTION	ENUMERATED BY ME ON THE ____ DAY OF _____, 1920		ENUMERATOR	

NAME	NATIVITY AND MOTHER TONGUE							ABLE TO SPEAK ENGLISH	OCCUPATION			NUMBER OF FARM SCHEDULE
	PLACE OF BIRTH OF EACH PERSON AND PARENTS OF EACH PERSON ENUMERATED. IF BORN IN U.S., GIVE STATE OR TERRITORY. IF FOREIGN BIRTH, GIVE THE PLACE OF BIRTH, AND, IN ADDITION, THE MOTHER TONGUE.											
	PERSON		FATHER		MOTHER							
OF EACH PERSON WHOSE PLACE OF ABODE ON JANUARY 1, 1920, WAS IN THIS FAMILY (from other side of form).	PLACE OF BIRTH	MOTHER TONGUE	PLACE OF BIRTH	MOTHER TONGUE	PLACE OF BIRTH	MOTHER TONGUE			TRADE, PROFESSION, OR PARTICULAR KIND OF WORK DONE.	INDUSTRY, BUSINESS, OR ESTABLISHMENT IN WHICH AT WORK.	EMPLOYER, SALARY OR WAGE WORKER, OR WORKING ON OWN ACCOUNT.	
5	19	20	21	22	23	24		25	26	27	28	29

15. Principal Meridians and Base Lines of the Federal System of Rectangular Surveys

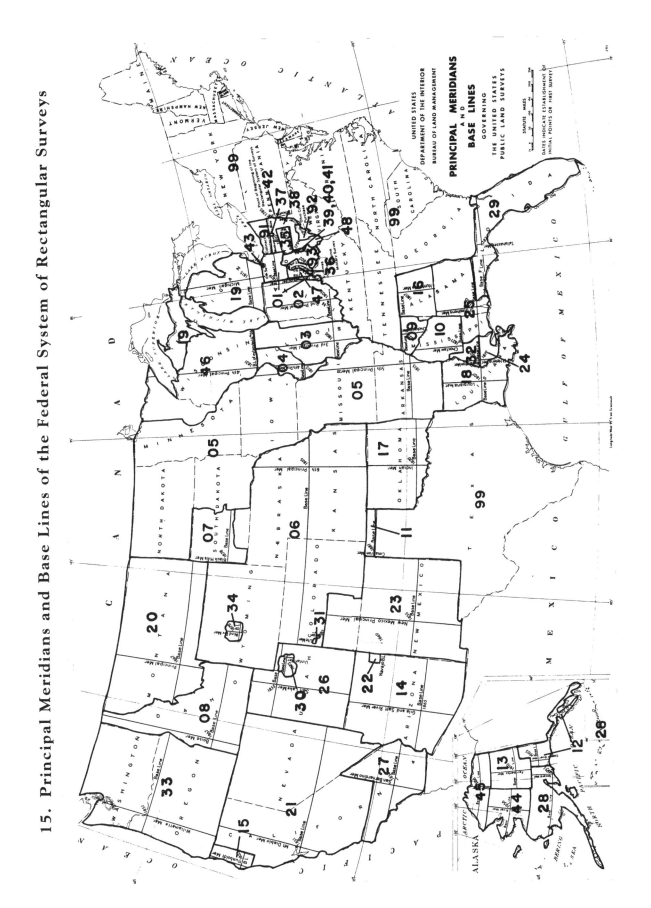

16. State Sources

Name: _____ Contact person: _____

Address: _____ Hours open: _____

Phone: _____ Photocopier available: _____

FAX: _____ Charges: _____

E-mail: _____ Notes: _____

Web site: _____ _____

Name: _____ Contact person: _____

Address: _____ Hours open: _____

Phone: _____ Photocopier available: _____

FAX: _____ Charges: _____

E-mail: _____ Notes: _____

Web site: _____ _____

Name: _____ Contact person: _____

Address: _____ Hours open: _____

Phone: _____ Photocopier available: _____

FAX: _____ Charges: _____

E-mail: _____ Notes: _____

Web site: _____ _____

Name: _____ Contact person: _____

Address: _____ Hours open: _____

Phone: _____ Photocopier available: _____

FAX: _____ Charges: _____

E-mail: _____ Notes: _____

Web site: _____ _____

Name: _____ Contact person: _____

Address: _____ Hours open: _____

Phone: _____ Photocopier available: _____

FAX: _____ Charges: _____

E-mail: _____ Notes: _____

Web site: _____ _____

Name: _____

Address: _____

Phone: _____

FAX: _____

E-mail: _____

Web site: _____

Contact person: _____

Hours open: _____

Photocopier available: _____

Charges: _____

Notes: _____

_____

Name: _____

Address: _____

Phone: _____

FAX: _____

E-mail: _____

Web site: _____

Contact person: _____

Hours open: _____

Photocopier available: _____

Charges: _____

Notes: _____

_____

Name: _____

Address: _____

Phone: _____

FAX: _____

E-mail: _____

Web site: _____

Contact person: _____

Hours open: _____

Photocopier available: _____

Charges: _____

Notes: _____

_____

Name: _____

Address: _____

Phone: _____

FAX: _____

E-mail: _____

Web site: _____

Contact person: _____

Hours open: _____

Photocopier available: _____

Charges: _____

Notes: _____

_____

Name: _____

Address: _____

Phone: _____

FAX: _____

E-mail: _____

Web site: _____

Contact person: _____

Hours open: _____

Photocopier available: _____

Charges: _____

Notes: _____

_____

17. County, City, Town, and Area Sources

Name: _____

Address: _____

Phone: _____

FAX: _____

E-mail: _____

Web site: _____

Contact person: _____

Hours open: _____

Photocopier available: _____

Charges: _____

Notes: _____

_____

Name: _____

Address: _____

Phone: _____

FAX: _____

E-mail: _____

Web site: _____

Contact person: _____

Hours open: _____

Photocopier available: _____

Charges: _____

Notes: _____

_____

Name: _____

Address: _____

Phone: _____

FAX: _____

E-mail: _____

Web site: _____

Contact person: _____

Hours open: _____

Photocopier available: _____

Charges: _____

Notes: _____

_____

Name: _____

Address: _____

Phone: _____

FAX: _____

E-mail: _____

Web site: _____

Contact person: _____

Hours open: _____

Photocopier available: _____

Charges: _____

Notes: _____

_____

Name: _____

Address: _____

Phone: _____

FAX: _____

E-mail: _____

Web site: _____

Contact person: _____

Hours open: _____

Photocopier available: _____

Charges: _____

Notes: _____

_____

Name: _____

Address: _____

Phone: _____

FAX: _____

E-mail: _____

Web site: _____

Contact person: _____

Hours open: _____

Photocopier available: _____

Charges: _____

Notes: _____

_____

Name: _____

Address: _____

Phone: _____

FAX: _____

E-mail: _____

Web site: _____

Contact person: _____

Hours open: _____

Photocopier available: _____

Charges: _____

Notes: _____

_____

Name: _____

Address: _____

Phone: _____

FAX: _____

E-mail: _____

Web site: _____

Contact person: _____

Hours open: _____

Photocopier available: _____

Charges: _____

Notes: _____

_____

Name: _____

Address: _____

Phone: _____

FAX: _____

E-mail: _____

Web site: _____

Contact person: _____

Hours open: _____

Photocopier available: _____

Charges: _____

Notes: _____

_____

Name: _____

Address: _____

Phone: _____

FAX: _____

E-mail: _____

Web site: _____

Contact person: _____

Hours open: _____

Photocopier available: _____

Charges: _____

Notes: _____

_____

18. Form 80—Order for Copies of Veterans Records

ORDER FOR COPIES OF VETERANS RECORDS
Please see Page 1 of this form for instructions.

Date Received (NNMS)

1. FILE TO BE SEARCHED (Check one box ONLY)

▶ ☐ PENSION   ☐ BOUNTY-LAND WARRANT APPLICATION (Service before 1856 only)

3 BRANCH OF SERVICE IN WHICH HE SERVED
☐ Army   ☐ Navy   ☐ Marine Corps   ☐ MILITARY

6 IF SERVICE WAS CIVIL WAR
☐ Union   ☐ Confederate

REQUIRED MINIMUM IDENTIFICATION OF VETERAN
Items 2, 3, 4, 5 (and 6 when applicable) MUST be completed or your order cannot be serviced.

2 VETERAN (Give last, first, and middle names)

4 STATE FROM WHICH HE SERVED

5 WAR IN WHICH, OR DATES BETWEEN WHICH HE SERVED

PLEASE PROVIDE THE FOLLOWING INFORMATION, IF KNOWN

7 UNIT IN WHICH HE SERVED (Name of regiment or number, company etc. name of ship)

8 IF SERVICE WAS ARMY, ARM IN WHICH HE SERVED
☐ Infantry   ☐ Cavalry   ☐ Artillery   If other, specify

9 KIND OF SERVICE
☐ Volunteers   ☐ Regulars

10 PENSION/BOUNTY-LAND FILE NO

11 IF VETERAN LIVED IN A HOME FOR SOLDIERS, GIVE LOCATION (City & State)

12 PLACE(S) VETERAN LIVED AFTER SERVICE

13 DATE OF BIRTH   14 PLACE OF BIRTH (City, County, State etc.)

15 DATE OF DEATH   16 PLACE OF DEATH (City, County, State, etc.)

17 NAME OF WIDOW OR OTHER CLAIMANT

Do NOT write below — Space is for our reply to you

☐ YES   We have located the file you requested above.   The cost is $5.00 for the file.

We have copied all or part of the file for you. Make your check or money order for $5.00, payable to **NATIONAL ARCHIVES TRUST FUND (NNMS).** Do NOT send cash. Return your payment **AND this invoice in the enclosed envelope. If the return envelope is missing,** send your payment **AND** this invoice to: Cashier (NJC), National Archives Trust Fund, 8th and Pennsylvania Avenue, NW, Washington, DC 20408. We must have this invoice to match your payment with your copies. WE WILL HOLD THESE COPIES AWAITING RECEIPT OF PAYMENT FOR 30 DAYS ONLY, FROM DATE STAMPED BELOW.

☐ NO   We were unable to locate the file you requested above.

☐ **REQUIRED MINIMUM IDENTIFICATION OF VETERAN WAS NOT PROVIDED.** Please complete items 2 (give full name), 3, 4, 5, and 6, and resubmit your order.

☐ **A SEARCH WAS MADE BUT THE FILE YOU REQUESTED ABOVE WAS NOT FOUND.** When we do not find a record for a veteran, this does not mean that he did not serve. You may be able to obtain information about him from the archives of the State from which he served.

☐ See attached forms, leaflets, or information sheets.

NNMS USE ONLY

SEARCHER   DATE

FILE DESIGNATION   781 834

▲ **THIS IS YOUR MAILING LABEL.** *Print your name (Last,*
First MI) and address within the block below. PRESS
FIRMLY - the information MUST appear on all copies.   **A**

NAME (Last, first, middle)

STREET

CITY   STATE   (Zip Code)

135

Index